ALCATRAZ ISLAND

Memoirs of a Rock Doc

Milton Daniel Beacher, M.D

Edited by Dianne Beacher Perfit

Pelican Island Publishing
Lebanon, New Jersey

This book is dedicated to the memory of Captain Gregory Lewis Beacher and Milton Daniel Beacher, M.D.

Published by:
Pelican Island Publishing
P. O. Box 671
Lebanon, NJ 08833
www.alcatrazdoc.com

Editor: Dianne Beacher Perfit
Photographs: Milton Daniel Beacher
Cover design: Gail Mardfin

Printed in the United States of America.

Library of Congress Control Number: 2001131911

ISBN: 0-9710332-0-X

www.alcatrazdoc.com

CONTENTS

Photographs

Poems

Note

Parenthetical comments and definitions throughout this book are attributed to the:
- Author when text appears in brackets.
- Editor when text appears in parentheses.

Dad taught me to type. He said it was an important skill to learn, even for a twelve-year-old. I remember him insisting on speed and accuracy. This was needed to transcribe his neat medical notations onto insurance forms or medical reports. He always found time to explain the words I typed, like hematoma – a big word for black and blue marks.

Little did I realize then the role typing would later play in my life. With a top speed of 87 words-per-minute, I ripped through many skill tests. This propelled me through the technology maze and into a career of technical writing, with some journalism mixed in for creative balance. Without these skills, editing and typing Dad's manuscript into my computer program would have been a major chore.

It wasn't. I relished each typed word. They seemed to jump off the computer screen and made me feel as if I was in the gray, misty fog at Alcatraz. His words became eloquent pictures of a dismal place with disheartened men.

Dad rarely discussed the prisoners or his experiences at Alcatraz. I knew he tried to publish the book in the 1950s. And there was some talk about a movie. Nothing materialized. My mother even appeared on a television program – would the panelists determine her secret? Shhh, she lived on the Rock during an escape!

One day when I was an adult, my father handed me his typed and bound manuscript. Large gold letters on the cover spelled *Alcatraz Island*. I was mesmerized by the stories. Periodically I would re-read the yellowing pages. Before his death in 1993, he asked me to fix it up and find a publisher. Publishers – big and small – were not interested. Disenchanted, his manuscript once again collected dust.

About six months ago, I felt compelled to revive this slice of history. I gave it a facelift, left the vivid descriptions that make the events so real and self-published the results. You actually hear the prisoners yammering during the strike and see prisoners Cole and Roe escape. Let me know if you see and hear these things, too.

Somehow I know that Dad is beaming down on me and cheering, "We finally did it!"

Enjoy. I did.

Dianne Beacher Perfit
Pelican Island Publishing
www.alcatrazdoc.com
April 26, 2001

P. S. Journal and bound manuscript were donated to the National Archives and Records Administration, San Bruno, California.

"Are you the new doc?" the guard on the pier demanded. I stared into a pair of cold, hard eyes and quickly responded, "Yes." He escorted me first to the dock office – where I signed the register – and then to a waiting car for a ride to the "top" where the fortress-like prison stood. Pointing to the straps hanging from the ceiling of the car, he suggested that I hold onto them. That was good advice. Each turn was so sharp and the hills so steep that I surely would have been thrown from my seat. It was on this ride that I first saw the prisoners.

Alcatraz Island was shrouded in mist and fog that April morning in 1937. The grayness had not lifted since my arrival earlier that day in San Francisco. When the Island finally peeked through the heaviness, it appeared flat, bleak and desolate. I was entranced. A smile of expectancy came to me – a feeling of adventure and excitement.

At the top, Dr. George Hess, the chief medical officer, and Warden Johnston awaited me in the Administration Building. Warden Johnston informed me of the absolute necessity to refrain from talking about Alcatraz to anyone on the mainland.

"We have nothing to hide," he said, "but we do not wish the institution to be the subject of discussion."

Then they fingerprinted me and took my picture with the same apparatus that did this same thing for every prisoner on Alcatraz. Unlike a prisoner, I was not surrounded by guards and was not being watched closely. I didn't feel exactly at home with so many steel-barred doors about me. This feeling emerged again later when I visited the men in isolation and solitary confinement. A solid door opened and a guard's flashlight played about the form rolled up in the blanket on the floor.

"Okay," he mumbled. The door was shut.

"That's Karpis," the guard explained. "Somebody smacked him out in the yard. What a shiner!"

I met Alvin Karpis again the next day when he was taken out of solitary confinement to have a tooth pulled by the visiting dentist. His left eye was black and blue. He was actually nervous about the tooth extraction.

Next, the notorious Al Capone came to see the dentist. He was much slimmer than any picture I had ever seen of him. His attitude was overbearingly friendly. I spoke to him at length.

The next day they showed me how to sit behind my desk during sick call. I was to sit with my chair rotated outward to the left away from the desk with my left foot outside the edge of the chair. In this position, I could quickly step back and out of reach should a prisoner decide to attack me.

My first patient arrived − a prisoner with a cinder in his eye.

"Fix my eye up, willya doc? I can hardly see," he pleaded.

He stood before me fully dressed in prison garb. He still wore his hat. I didn't notice this and if I did it wouldn't have made any difference to me. But the guard saw it.

"Take your hat off," he demanded. "How dare you stand there and talk to the doctor with your hat on." The prisoner removed his hat.

My work at Alcatraz had begun.

My father sailed to Alcatraz Island aboard the Gen. F.M. Coxe launch. It was only a ten-minute cruise from the Fort Mason pier in San Francisco to the Alcatraz dock.

A journal entry described the streetcar ride to the pier as "fast and furious. I expected the car to leave the tracks at any moment."

Trying to find the pier was difficult – not even the police could help. My father resorted to calling Dr. Hess at Alcatraz for directions. A guard relayed the directions from Dr. Hess because on Alcatraz "no direct communication or conversation" was allowed.

Devil's Island

The lights of "Broadway," the main corridor in the Alcatraz cellblock, blazed brilliantly as they did nightly. Bed springs squeaked as an occasional prisoner tossed restlessly in his sleep. Blatant snores echoed through the cellblock. One of the guards on duty stiffened when he heard a thud, then a pause. Then followed a series of thuds, spaced with pauses.

He tiptoed down the cellblock, tracing the sound. When he came to the cell of Joe Kalinoski, he gasped. Kalinoski was on his hands and knees on the floor. His head was matted with blood. Like a charging bull, snorting and head down, Kalinoski was butting his head against the concrete cell wall.

Red welts on the wall showed the many times he butted his head. He would sink to the floor in momentary unconsciousness, then stumble back to his hands and knees and smash into the wall again. He was brought to the hospital in a daze. "I only wanted to knock the noises out of my head, doc," he muttered as I administered a sedative.

Another prisoner, Joe Bowers "wanted out." Bowers, a post office robber, tried suicide by slashing his throat with a razor blade. His unsuccessful suicide attempt produced a superficial wound. Prison psychiatrists termed his suicide attempt "theatrically planned, resulting in very little damage to himself." Bowers was termed "not a normal individual, but not so crazy as he was trying to make out."

Bowers tended the incinerator and shoveled the Alcatraz garbage into it. It was an outside job. The chilly San Francisco Bay wind whipped and fluttered his uniform. Below, white-capped waves dashed themselves to bits against the jagged rocks. Between Bowers and the waves stood a towering, barbed wire fence and the constant scrutiny of tower guards.

One afternoon, Bowers dropped his shovel and walked doggedly toward the fence. He inched his way up. Barbed wire gouged into his hands and ripped his clothes. But he kept climbing, higher, higher. A tower guard spotted him and shouted a warning. Bowers kept climbing. Whammmm! A shot cracked from the guard tower. It plowed into his chest. He teetered. Whammm! A second bullet hit him. He hurtled seventy-five feet to the water's edge, amid the jagged rocks.

I saw them retrieve his broken, lifeless body. Bowers, who wanted out, got it the next day. Strapped on a stretcher, a gray prison blanket pulled up over his face, he was shipped to the San Francisco morgue. I heard his fellow prisoners say, "No, Joe Bowers didn't try to escape. He committed suicide all right. He knew he couldn't make it over the fence with the guards eyeing him. But he figured it was a better way out than using a razor blade."

And then there was Rufe Persful. He plodded along for months working on the garbage detail, removing garbage from the Alcatraz residences. Then he got to thinking.

"Hey, Parker, jump off that seventy-foot wall," he urged his partner one day. "Don't stand there asking me why. I just want to see if you'd break in half."

That afternoon Persful obtained an axe and carried it to a chopping block. As though about to chop some kindling, he kneeled, put his left hand squarely on the chopping block and swung the axe with his right hand, smashing it down on the flat hand. He severed four complete fingers and half the palm. The blow was so hard that the axe split the wood block. Guards ran up and yanked the axe away. Persful begged them to hack off his right hand. When they refused, he sneered, "Ah, ain't you guys got any guts?"

These were only a few instances of the suicidal antics that Alcatraz witnessed in increasing numbers. Maniacal laughter was heard daily in the hospital. Outsiders didn't know that men were cracking mentally. Not until news trickled out that Capone, their most famous prisoner, had "blown his top."

Why were prisoners blowing their tops on the dreaded Devil's Island?

First, there was the noise – the forlorn moans of the Alcatraz foghorn – the melancholy swish of the waves – the incessant clomp-clomp and scuffle of the guards' hob-nailed boots – the whirring, thwacking, thumping clatter in the prison shops – the incessant CLANG, CLANG, CLANG of bells that jolted prisoners into action. CLANG, CLANG, CLANG, time to get up. CLANG, CLANG,

CLANG, time to march to the mess hall. CLANG, CLANG, CLANG, time for another checkup count.

And the constant banging and bumping of cell doors.

And the fog – melancholy, depressing, gray, swirling.

And the deadly monotony – endlessly stitching strips of cut-up tires into mat forms. Stitch-stitch-stitch until the fingers ached. Or feeding vast quantities of Army transport linen into the maw of an electric washer. Dirty shorts, dirty undershirts, dirty sheets, and dirty pillowcases. Dozens upon dozens, feed it in, feed it in. Or, hunched over a whirring machine in the tailor shop, grinding out coats, coats, coats.

And there was the no-talking rule. "They might just as well cut off a guy's tongue, for the amount of gab they let him spill here," they often complained to me. There was no talking in the mess hall, except to whisper, "Pass the salt." And there was no talking in the cellblock. So what did a prisoner do between lockup time and lights out at 9:30 p.m.?

He tried to read. He tried to write. He squirmed and writhed. He wanted to talk – to feel words spill out of his throat, to hear the voice of someone, anyone, from an adjoining cell. Companionship – he was groping for companionship. But the other occupants of the cellblock lay in their cots silent and motionless, like bodies in steel and concrete crypts. And there was no silence, for about them was the braying foghorn, the splashing waves, and the shuffling boots.

Of course, the lack of privileges made life more miserable. No radios. No newspapers. No movies, except on legal holidays. No commissary, where candy or cookies could be bought, like in other prisons. There was only the cheap, harsh tobacco the government provided that gave them some solace. And on weekends there was the brief recreation time, when they ran, jumped and cavorted in the yard until CLANG, CLANG, CLANG sent them back to their crypts.

The harsh discipline made men bitter. The dungeon and solitary confinement cells were always open to misbehaving prisoners. And if a prisoner went on a hunger strike to protest something, he had a rubber tube jammed down his throat or nostrils and was forcibly fed. Time and again, I force-fed striking prisoners.

And finally, there was enforced maximum security, led by the continuous swirling, dangerous tides — tool-proof steel — barbed wire hedges — and the tower guards patrolling restlessly. All this along with the tear gas "chandeliers" in the mess hall and cellblock, guards with tear gas billys (metal container with a leather handle, the size of a police club, containing tear gas cartridges), and the continuous shakedowns (searches) for contraband, missing articles, and concealed weapons. All this added to their hopelessness.

Was this new drastic American prison a success, with its rigid discipline and no babying or coddling?

Alcatraz Island, America's Devil's Island, turned numerous prisoners into babbling mad men, necessitating their transfer to mental institutions.

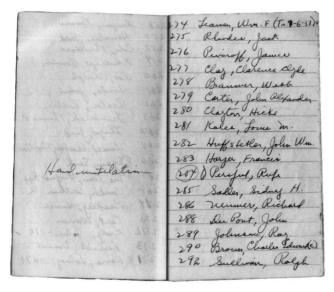

This is a page from my father's handwritten roster, noting that prisoner 284 – Rufe Persful – mutilated his hand.

Rufe Persful lay for hours in his hospital cot reading a small Bible and muttering to himself. He was transferred here after mutilating his hand.

"See, doc," he said, pointing to cracks in the wall, "those are roads. At night people come down those roads. They flock around a big oasis, beneath palm trees, and listen to me preach."

One night he put down his Bible and crept out of bed. He tiptoed to an adjoining bed where another prisoner lay in a restraining jacket. Persful stared at him intently. Then he ripped off the wire from the electric pad on the stump of his hand and fashioned a noose. Wagging the noose in front of the other prisoner, Persful whispered zealously,

"Brother, wilt thou be converted and saved from hell fire and brimstone? Yea, verily, thou shalt sizzle in Hades, unless thou recognize the error of thy ways. Come, I shall forgive thee thy trespasses."

The other prisoner was sleeping and mumbled something incoherently.

"Verily, I shall proceed with my ritual of conversion – I shall purify thy soul," Persful grunted.

He placed the noose about the other prisoner's neck, holding the cord in his right hand. He reached for his Bible, opened it, and began intoning,

"Brothers and sisters, here lies Judas who snitched on Jesus Christ for thirty cents in silver."

And with a jerk that jolted the prisoner completely awake, Persful yanked on the wire, tightening the improvised noose. Persful repeated his words.

"Brothers and sisters, here lies Judas who snitched on Jesus Christ for thirty cents in silver." And again he jerked the wire, tightening the noose. The other prisoner's eyes bulged. He screamed. Guards ran in and separated them. Persful stomped away, angry.

"Aw, I was making a sacrifice and converting him," he scowled. "Then you guys had to come in."

Persful was moved to a separate cell. Several days later he called me aside and held up another noose, made from an electric extension cord.

"See, doc, this is a hanging knot," he beamed. "It's a legal knot, too. It's got 13 turns in it." I took it away from him.

At intervals he was allowed to mingle with other patients in the hospital. He used the time to convert them. They ignored him. Then Persful would trudge back to his cell and mope.

"They don't believe me, doc," he sighed. "None of the goddamned people around here believe. They say I'm not a preacher and a prophet. These damn bastards in the cages next to me don't believe anything. The world is round, isn't it? That's what I've been telling them, but they don't believe me. They tell me it's flat and has foursquare corners on it. And there ain't no such goddamn thing."

Persful, who was doing twenty years for a minor kidnapping, was in his early thirties. He loathed psychiatric examinations.

"Did you ever hobo?" he was asked.

"Sure."

"Do you know what a hobo is?"

"Sure, a tramp."

"Whom did you hobo with?"

"Nobody. Always by myself."

"Why did you want to stay by yourself all the time?"

"If I go with somebody, trouble starts and you end up in jail."

"Do you want to go to jail?"

"No, SIR! Man, you must think I'm crazy."

"What year is this, Persful?"

"Thirteen hundred and thirteen."

"Isn't it 1938?"

"Yes."

"Why is 1313 on your mind?"

"I don't know. But my birthday is May 13. And I was hanged in 1313. And I'm going to be born again."

"Do you believe that?"

"Sure. I'm a preacher and I believe in God. Don't you believe in God? Man, if you don't believe in God you sure are messed up."

"Of course I believe in God, Persful. What church do you belong to?"

"I don't belong to any. I'm just a preacher. What kind of a man are you?"

"Just an ordinary man. What do you preach?"

"I ain't saying. I ain't holding church now. I preach at night."

"Is your mother living?"

"No. She got her head chopped off."

"Is your father living?"

"No. He got hanged. I'm gonna get hanged too, and I'm gonna be born again."

"What happened to your hand?"

"Well, it was an accident. I ain't telling. It was just an ordinary accident."

"Did you ever have other accidents?"

"What you asking me all them questions for? Man, you must think I'm crazy. I ain't saying nothing else. That's all. I want to go back to my cell."

Persful had an inherent sardonic humor. A guard accompanied him to the prison bathroom and gave him a blade to shave with. Presently Persful came out and walked across the ward to his cell, unshaven.

"Why didn't you shave?" the guard asked.

"Oh," Persful smiled, "I have no blade."

"But you were given one."

Persful feigned surprise.

"Why, no!"

The hospital staff and guards were called. A loose razor blade was extremely dangerous. Persful was questioned at length.

"But I haven't got it." Pointing to a guard, he said, "He has it."

"What would he want it for?"

"He has a mustache. Maybe he wants to shave it off. He ought to. He looks awful with it."

It was night. Additional guards were summoned to search for the missing blade. The hospital patients were roused and lined up in the middle of the ward. Each one was stripped and searched. Then the hospital was literally taken apart. Crannies, shelves, closets, loose boards – everything was searched. Screwdrivers tore apart cabinets and other pieces of furniture. Sacks of tobacco were emptied on the floor. Bed sheets and mattresses were thoroughly searched. After a frantic search, the blade was found in a large receptacle in which bedpans were emptied. Throughout the entire search, Persful grinned at the commotion he was causing.

Several days later, Persful walked over to me and asked confidentially,

"Doc, can people see things that aren't here? I didn't want to tell you because you wouldn't believe me. But I'm not lying this time."

"Sure, Persful. What did you see?"

"Well, I saw an animal come out of the washbasin and slide along the floor. It was a big alligator, doc. Just as big as that bed. It was long and slimy and had scales with moss on it. It had big red eyes and teeth that long. I was so scared I couldn't even yell."

"What did you do?"

"Nothing. I just lay in bed and it went away. I knew it wasn't real because it wasn't working its hind legs. But I've seen other things, too. The other day a man was in here sitting on my chest for three hours and I couldn't get him off. Last night a man pulled my hair. I'll tell you, doc, I don't like my room – it's dark in there. I don't sleep so well."

Despite his condition, Persful was still able to size up his fellow hospital patients. He spotted one patient who had an apparent paralysis of the left leg and maneuvered about on crutches. This prisoner was suspected of malingering. Persful suspected it, too. One afternoon, as Persful was going to the bathroom with a urinal, he met this prisoner at the door. The other prisoner hesitated.

"Come on, come on," Persful urged.

The other prisoner gave a taunting reply. Persful then sloshed a full urinal over him. Intervention by attendants prevented further fighting. Later the other prisoner crossed the ward, picked up a milk bottle and heaved it at Persful, who was in the far end of the room. It barely missed Persful. Incensed, Persful sprinted into the bathroom, bounded out with his urinal, and chased the other prisoner. The "paralyzed" prisoner dropped his crutches and crawled nimbly under the bed, screaming for help. Persful bent down and walloped him over the head with the urinal.

"Persful," I asked after the pair had been separated again, "aren't you ashamed for hitting a cripple?"

"Huh," Persful grunted. "He isn't as crippled as you think he is."

It was unpleasant to watch once able-bodied men end up as babbling, demoniac mad men. Such was the case with Joe Kalinoski, the prisoner who butted his head against the cell wall.

Kalinoski was a model prisoner. He obeyed the bell signals and the guards' whistles. He always stood by his cell door for regular checkups. Then the drastic Alcatraz regime began to prey on his mind, to frazzle his nerves. In the long, silent hours of solitude, visions began swirling before his eyes.

He began to imagine being called a "stoolie" by the other prisoners.

Kalinoski lay on his cot as the foghorn brayed outside and tried to tell himself over and over he was a "right guy." But something in his mind kept repeating incessantly,

"Joe Kalinoski, you're a stoolie."

One morning, as the prisoners started trudging to the mess hall, Kalinoski bolted from the line. He refused to march or eat with the others because he was a stoolie, an outsider, and not an equal.

Another day, when a prisoner chanced to speak with him, Kalinoski threw himself at the prisoner. Both men were placed in solitary confinement for fighting.

"Why did you strike that man?" Kalinoski was asked.

"I thought he called me a stool pigeon. The others always call me that."

"Are you 'stooling' on anybody?"

"No."

"Then why are they calling you a stool pigeon?"

Kalinoski fidgeted. An appealing look came to his eyes. He shrugged his shoulders and sobbed,

"I don't know . . . I don't know. I don't understand it."

"A few days in solitary might make you understand it," was the answer.

Kalinoski left solitary confinement haggard, wan and more fearful than ever. He was always afraid that if he went into the mess hall, the other prisoners would gang up on him and beat him.

"Kalinoski's a stoolie – Kalinoski's a stoolie!" Like little white maggots, the thought ate into his mind. He imagined himself just about the most despised thing on the Island – a stool pigeon.

Finally he appealed to me.

"They're calling me a squealer. I think it's because of a letter I once wrote," he wailed. "Let me go to isolation for awhile, doc. Maybe I'll feel better. I don't feel so good now. I don't know what it is but I hear noises in my head. When I talk the words are repeated after me. But I don't know who says them. When I read, the words are repeated after me, too."

"Don't you think it's just your imagination, Kalinoski?"

"Oh no. I hear those voices, just as I hear your voice now. I know somebody is talking. But still that can't be – how can voices be talking when there's no one around? It just isn't right. It sounds crazy. That's why I want to go to isolation, where I can be by myself."

Isolation brought no improvement. Then, like a dam that stands the buffeting of surging water only to crumble, Kalinoski's mind cracked wide open. And that's when he bruised and battered himself almost beyond recognition to "get the noises out of my head." He was placed in a straight jacket. And there he lay, his hair matted with blood, his lips swollen, his eyes blackened, his cheeks and chin bruised and scraped to a pulp, whimpering and shrieking in torment, fear, and agony.

"Help! Help! Let me out of here – they're coming to get me – I'm a stoolie."

His tortured mind was playing tricks. Kalinoski was alone.

Gray-clad prisoners shuffled to work and played in the yard during the recreation hour. No one knew when one would suddenly crack in the midst of the day's routine. Harold June's turn came when he refused to line up with the other prisoners.

"Get back in line, June!" commanded a guard.

"I want to get that goddam radio up there," June retorted.

"There's no radio up there."

"Sure there is. It's up there near the ceiling. It was left over by the Army."

"You needn't worry about that – get back in line."

From then on, June changed rapidly. It became necessary to put him in isolation. For several months, he busied himself with childish play, making all sorts of things in his cell or piling his belongings in peculiar fashion in the middle of the floor and balancing things on top of the heap. Other times he became boisterous. Jerking open his collar, he clutched at his throat and gasped for air, shouting, "I want out of this goddam place! It's hot. It's a hot box. I'm suffocating. See that hole up there? Electricity is coming from it. I'LL GET ELECTROCUTED!"

It was the repetition of these outbursts that finally brought him to the prison hospital.

"I'm an American citizen," he screamed. "I want justice. I was raised in a home for the feeble-minded, but I'm not crazy. I ran away and joined the Army and became a muleskinner. That's what I want to do around here, if you only had some mules."

He punctuated his words with a considerable racket, made by sloshing his tin water cup and urinal against the bars. Despite his pleadings and violent efforts to prevent it, we placed him in a straight jacket. Tears streamed down his cheeks. Like a frightened child pleading not to be spanked, he cried, "Don't tie me up – I'll be good – please don't tie me up."

There were occasional lulls when his seething mind calmed. And when these periods of calm and restfulness came, June was happy and contented, and his voice rang out in song. Then he abruptly reverted to his turbulent antics. During one period of destruction, he tore a bed sheet into narrow strips and wound them into a ball.

"Here's a ball I made, doc," he grinned. "Don't look at it until you get home."

I took it, of course. A short time later the ball was thoroughly unwound and the loose strips given to him again – it was cheaper than letting him wreck havoc with a new sheet each time.

Other times he delighted in reading magazines and looking at pictures upside down. He intently eyed a picture and reflected knowingly,

"Now, that guy's a criminal, doc. Just look at his eyes. And see this kid. That's the worst type of criminal. I can tell just by looking at him."

June delighted in drawing pictures of little people by making a circle for the head and straight lines for the body and the extremities.

"Hey, take this," he would grin childishly, handing an attendant a piece of crumpled cigarette paper. "Now, don't look at it until you get home." And then he laughed long and heartily.

Upon examination, the paper showed pictures of his little people in various positions.

He continually messed up his cell, heaving clothes and blankets around. Many times, like an agile chimpanzee, he climbed up the bars to the ceiling, and hung there, grimacing at those who passed below. His cell resembled the fire escape of a tenement – sheets, blankets and towels were suspended from the bars. All his personal belongings, such as cup, toothbrush, shaving brush, and blue handkerchief, were tied around his body with his pajama string. And with his belongings dangling about him, he would hippity-hop about, like something in a zoo.

"Monkey," he grinned, wagging his cup and acting docile. But other times he played gorilla. Scowling, eyes narrowed into fierce slits, he jutted his jaw forward and tore his bed sheets, roared, and tormented other prisoners with vile, crazy language, incoherent sentences, and guttural barking. Guards hastened to quiet him.

A scuffle ensued, with June kicking and biting and yelling, "Don't hurt me." Subdued, he squatted on his haunches and watched the attendants clean up his cell.

Attendants removed the blankets, cup, books, mattress, and loose paraphernalia. When June saw his two Bibles being swept out, he became infuriated.

"You goddam heathens," he roared. "Take those Bibles off the floor. Ain't you got no respect for nothing?"

And then he lashed out at the attendants. A guard pinned his arms and held him up against the cell wall. Not until the Bibles were restored would he be quiet. That night, while the other hospital patients were asleep, June played gorilla again. Pounding his urinal against the bars and wall, he smashed a hole in the plaster, clear down to the lathe.

Guards were summoned to quiet him. They found a raging beast. Talking to him was futile. A guard fired a gas pellet into the cell. Smoke swirled upward, engulfing June. Coughing and gasping for breath, tears streaming down his face, he dangled from the bars at the top of his cell. Then, unable to stand it any longer, he climbed down and was quiet. The next day, he swore that the guard gassed him to make him unconscious and commit sodomy.

Shuffle-shuffle-shuffle. Lines of prisoners marched back to their cells after lunch. Everything was orderly and precise. Then, from a cell on the third tier, came yowling and screeching. Webb Brammer was blowing his top.

Arms laden with everything movable in his cell, Brammer lunged to the railing and started heaving the objects on the prisoners marching below.

As a final gesture, he yanked out the wooden shelf in his cell and flung it down. It hurtled through the air, struck with a resounding crash and barely missed a guard.

Since his incarceration at Alcatraz, Brammer shirked virtually every type of work. He was hospitalized numerous times to better his physical condition, particularly his disposition, which was bitter. He seemed destined to spend the rest of his days in misery. He expressed no desire to work or to help himself. Marching to the mess hall or to the work area, he always lagged behind, leaving a wide gap between himself and the man in front.

Because of his insolence and his refusal to work, he was slapped into isolation for four weeks. The "cure" failed to work. It made him more bitter.

On emerging from isolation, Brammer developed a chronic complaint. Everything possible was done to relieve him of his magnified pain, but to no avail.

While in the hospital after his cellblock outburst, Brammer went berserk again. He stared at a wall clock in the ward for hours. As his eyes followed the to-and-fro motion of the pendulum, he muttered,

"Tick – tick – tick. Twenty-five years. Tick – tick – tick. Twenty-five years. That's what I gotta do. Go on, TICK! Tick faster, can't you? TICK FASTER, I SAY! Finish ticking off twenty-five years so I can get to hell out of here."

His only response was the slow, rhythmic ticking. It went on, oblivious to his command. Angered, he yelled, picked up a small stool and heaved it at the clock. Glass tinkled, the clock swung sideways and the pendulum halted abruptly.

"That's one way of beating your time here," a passing prisoner tittered.

I visited Brammer in his isolation cell, where he was transferred. He sat huddled on his bed, a blanket around his shoulders, and a wet towel tied around his forehead. In the days that followed, he imagined himself to be a block of marble. He refused to speak or even answer questions. He was content to lie on his cot and stare at the ceiling.

On my night rounds, I inquired how he was feeling. There was no response. I inserted my hand through the bars, and then shook the bed, fearing that he might have suffocated. Brammer lay face down. I grabbed his head and turned him face up. Assured that he was all right, I walked away.

Then followed some sort of game between Brammer and the guards. He would throw the mattress off his cot and sleep on the floor. After several days of this, the guards decided the mattress was to go on the cot again. Brammer protested.

"I'm going to sleep on the floor," he declared.

"No, you're not," the guards insisted.

"I am!"

"You're not."

Then the game began. In order to lift the mattress onto the cot, the guards had to push Brammer off. Once the mattress was on the bed, they lifted Brammer – stiff as a piece of marble – off the floor and onto the bed. He absolutely refused to move by himself. An hour later, when the guards made their rounds again, they found Brammer contentedly lying on the floor.

Screams. Crash. Tinkle. Breaking medicine bottles. Ripping sounds of clothing and blankets. Thwacking noise of a wooden shelf being banged against the bars. The din echoed throughout the cellblock. Prisoners leapt from their cots where they were resting or reading, leaned against the cell doors, and thrust their heads out. Who blew his top this time, they wondered? Later they learned it was Fred Reese.

"The other cons don't like me," he confided to me in the hospital. "They don't talk to me. They don't pass me anything at the table when I ask them to. When they eat they save their scraps of food for me and take my good food away. Besides, I don't get my mail – they keep that from me, too. I've got a sweetheart outside and all I have to live for is her letters. Why do they want to keep her letters from me, doc?"

The fear that other prisoners hated them was one of the commonest delusions on Alcatraz.

With prisoners periodically blowing their tops, most looked askance at who they worked next to in the shops, who they sat next to in the mess hall, and who they played sports with in the yard during recreation periods. Fellow prisoners who suddenly went berserk attacked many innocent bystanders.

Cal Young was such an innocent bystander.

Young was watching a prison ballgame when the man next to him turned and, without provocation, bit him on the forehead, cheek and finger. A severe infection followed on Young's finger, resulting in the loss of his nail.

William E. Colyer was Young's attacker. Colyer committed a murder while serving in the Army. He was sent to Leavenworth from Germany and arrived there just before Christmas 1920. He maintained he had nothing to do with the murder, that he was drunk at the time and knew nothing of the affair. At Leavenworth, he was in isolation for a considerable time. He created disturbances by yelling, cutting up, and banging his bed up and down.

"I joined the Army because people were always doing things to me, and talking about me," he whimpered. "I figured in the Army I would be protected. But they persecuted me, even there."

At Leavenworth his persecution ideas centered on the warden. He charged that the warden kept framing him, made him miserable, and was responsible for preventing his clemency from Washington. Diagnosed as having a definite paranoid psychosis, he was transferred to St. Elizabeth's Hospital in Washington, D.C. in 1930. He was returned to Leavenworth the following year. Then came Alcatraz.

What became of the Alcatraz prisoner who went berserk? The Rock didn't have the necessary equipment to handle them, so they were transferred to the federal institution for the mentally ill in Springfield, Missouri. True, some prisoners feigned their insanity. Others were malingerers who used it as an opportunity to escape work. Hence, a transfer board met at Alcatraz whenever necessary.

The board consisted of the chief medical officer at Alcatraz and two San Francisco psychiatrists. They questioned the alleged insane prisoner and determined his condition. If it warranted transfer, they wrote their findings and gave them to the chief medical officer. He made a summary of these findings and sent them to Washington with the transfer request. Usually within a few weeks, Washington sent orders to Alcatraz for the transfer.

Number 47 was escaping from Alcatraz. Yet the prison floodlights weren't on, turning the night into day. Guards weren't scurrying about, firing gas cartridges into the caves and crannies to ferret him out. Coast Guard patrol boats weren't radioed to stretch a blockade around the Rock. Nor was the escape siren screeching.

Number 47, Edward Wutke, sat upright in his cell as his life drained out in sluggish red trickles. Wutke was bleeding to death, a suicide, gritting his teeth, steeling himself to choke off the slightest moan or whimper that might attract the attention of the guards on duty.

His lethal weapon dangled in his fingers – the tiny blade of a pencil sharpener screwed into place in a safety razor. When the lights out bell clanged at 9:30 p.m., Wutke prepared for his rendezvous with death. Clutching the improvised razor, he climbed into bed and pulled the blankets over his face. A few minutes later he heard the pounding of boots. Wutke heard the guard halt at his cell and knew he was peering in. Then the pounding continued down the cellblock and died away.

The only sound now was the sighing and sloshing of the restless surf outside. With blankets still high over his neck, Wutke started hacking at his jugular vein. It must have been painful – the pencil sharpener blade was blunt.

Methodically he kept hacking away, the thin scratches of his first attempts turning into jagged gashes. He finally produced a wound on each side of his neck about three inches long and one and one-half inches deep. The jugular vein was severed. Blood coursed down his neck, drenching the blankets and the mattress. He forced himself to sit upright, thinking that he would bleed to death quicker.

As the blood gurgled out of his neck and he felt himself grow weaker, what thoughts surged through his mind? Did the swishing of the waves outside remind him of his sea-going days?

At 17, Wutke went to sea and followed it steadily until he was sentenced to Alcatraz for murder. On that last fateful voyage, his ship had lain over in San Diego for many days. He spent the time drinking heavily with a shipmate.

They staggered back to the ship, arm in arm. Wutke invited his companion to have a drink in his cabin. Then things went hazy in his memory. All he could recollect later was that he had groped his way on deck to perform his regular duties when the ship cast off. Later he awoke in the ship's washroom. By its rocking and throbbing, he knew they were underway. Something hard was biting into his wrists. Groggily, he forced his eyes open and saw he was in irons.

Eventually he was told what happened. When they ran out of liquor, the shipmate went to his cabin and got more. He refused to share it with Wutke. A scuffle ensued. In the drunken brawl, Wutke stabbed the shipmate in the groin with a knife. The ship was several hours out of port and the shipmate bled to death before they returned to port. And now Wutke was bleeding to death, too.

The government charged Wutke with murder on the high seas. Murder on the high seas! It sounded romantic. It conjured up visions of mutineers, of faded, creased maps and buried treasure. Wutke was sentenced to 27 years on Alcatraz. To a man who loved the sea with its vastness and changing moods, confinement was unbearable. All about him on Alcatraz was the blue – sometimes gray – sea. From his cell he could see freighters and luxury liners heading in and out of the Golden Gate.

Wutke yearned for the feel of salt spray against his cheeks, a swaying ship under his feet, and distant horizons. When the longing became unbearable, his thoughts turned to suicide. He tried it once before and even sought a weapon. But Alcatraz officials removed all possible suicide weapons from the cells. So Wutke hit upon the idea of the blade in the pencil sharpener. Taking the sharpener apart, he extracted the tiny blade.

It was only about an inch long and three-eighths of an inch wide. Awkwardly, Wutke grasped the tiny weapon in his pudgy fingers and started to saw his left arm, at the bend of the elbow. The inflicted wound was not deep, but he bled profusely. A cell guard noticed him and brought Wutke to the hospital. I sutured the wound. Wutke, on this occasion, begged to have his life saved. Perhaps he realized that he would not die, and wanted to throw off any suspicion that he was still despondent. He recovered and returned to work, vowing at great length that he would make no further attempts at suicide.

Some months later he was successful at the job he had once bungled. That night, a guard passed Wutke's cell and saw the blood pool on the bed. Prison officials, including myself, were called.

"Well, he's dead," I said after a brief examination. "The morgue will be his new cell for the night."

The deputy warden called for a stretcher. The body that was Edward Wutke was wrapped in a blanket and carried to the morgue.

"Say, deputy," the cellhouse guard asked, "what shall I do about the checkup count? Shall I include Wutke in it?"

"Yes. Every man on the Island must be accounted for, dead or alive. Wutke will be discharged by death when he leaves Alcatraz in the morning."

At noon the following day, Wutke went on his last voyage. Salt spray plumed upward, the boat throbbed and rocked. He was taken by launch to the San Francisco morgue. Wutke had escaped Alcatraz.

The horror of serving long-term sentences amidst the drab monotony of Alcatraz life put thoughts of suicide into the minds of despondent prisoners. But how could it be done painlessly and easily? The usual methods of suicide were not available. Poison? It was kept locked in the prison hospital. Leaping from great heights? Let a prisoner go somewhere where he didn't belong and at least six guards halted him. Razors? Safety razor blades were meted out and gathered after use. Gas? It wasn't available, either.

Joe Bowers – referred to previously – died from a gunshot wound. Instead of inflicting it himself, he feigned an escape, well knowing that a bullet would stop him as he started climbing the fence. Other prisoners preferred to commit suicide in the solitude of their cells, alone.

That was the case of Robert Jones, serving a life term for murder. He was transferred to Alcatraz from Leavenworth. While on the Rock, he was suspected of having homosexual relations with another prisoner. There was no actual proof. Both prisoners were kept under close scrutiny. The constant surveillance produced an emotional reaction in Jones' companion, culminating in a hysterical attack. When Jones learned of his friend's condition, he became unnerved and began to weep.

I was awakened at 12:30 a.m. and called to the cellhouse. I found Jones unconscious on the floor. Blood was splattered about the cell. His breathing was labored. A hasty examination showed he made superficial cuts on both wrists. Later I found he did this with a pin that he used to hold up his pants.

Further examination showed he swallowed a bottle of soap liniment I had given him. He apparently drank the liniment, cut his wrists, stuffed a handkerchief down his throat, and proceeded to hang himself from the bars with his belt. Unconscious, he fell to the floor. The thud attracted the attention of the guard. If not for this thud, his attempt would have been successful.

I removed the handkerchief from his throat. Then the guard helped me get Jones out of the cell, as I wished to take him to the hospital. While the guard was closing the cell door, Jones came to life and began to fight with the fury of a panther. He attempted to dive under the railing to the floor below. He succeeded in squirming and wriggling practically his entire body off the landing, with the exception of one foot. I grabbed his foot, and was frantically hanging on, trying to hold him back.

There I was, sitting on the floor, holding onto one leg to prevent him from making the dive, and bracing myself against the railing with my feet. The guard sprinted to my aid and we pulled Jones onto the landing.

All the way to the hospital, Jones cowered and cringed like a frightened animal. He was not fully conscious and kept mumbling, "It's all right – it won't be long now – it'll be over soon – swing low, sweet chariot, I'll be ridin' in you soon." Jones thought he was still in his cell, dangling from the bars.

When he became fully conscious and realized what happened, he broke down and cried like a baby. He was kept in the hospital under observation for 21 days. A week after his attempted suicide, I questioned him, asking why he did it. He replied he 'just felt bad,' and said that he wouldn't try it again.

After his discharge from the hospital, Jones made a complete recovery from his emotional breakdown and became a model prisoner.

Although lethal weapons were difficult to improvise, prisoners devised innovative gadgets from innocent-appearing furnishings in their cells.

John Stadig disconnected a light bulb in his cell. He used the metal band around it in knife fashion, but it proved too blunt. Undaunted, he stepped on the bulb, broke it, and started hacking at his body with glass slivers. He was detected and transferred to Springfield. A short time after he arrived there, he died a suicide.

Blankets and sheets were frequently used as nooses. Mack Stroud, alias Ed Jackson, was serving 25 years for violation of the post office laws, assault and robbery. He attempted to hang himself in his cell but the sheet was found – not around his neck – but around his jaw. One foot was on the bed, as if he was protecting himself from falling. Evidently he didn't have the courage to go through with it. Several weeks later he made another, more determined attempt. This time the sheet was firmly tied around his neck, and he was unconscious when found. Had he not been promptly cut down, he no doubt would have strangled.

Prison garb was even used in a suicide try. Cecil Snow, serving 15 years for post office theft, decided to end his life before the evening meal. Snow ripped his gray coveralls into strips and proceeded to strangle himself by hanging from the bars. Two guards found him unconscious. One held him and the other cut him down with a pocketknife.

"Why do you want to commit suicide?" I asked him in the prison hospital.

"Doctor," he replied, "I'm not in a physical condition to work. I can't make it in this hole. I just decided to end it all."

"Did you think you could get away with it?"

"I wouldn't have tried it if I thought I wouldn't."

Summoned to appear before the deputy warden, Snow was informed he was being sent back to work and that all his privileges would be taken away until further notice.

"If you don't behave and don't work, the dungeon will be waiting for you," he was told.

"Okay," Snow said meekly, "I'll work."

The lament, "I can't make my time," was the commonest explanation prisoners gave for attempting suicide. A typical example was Arlen Wylie, who was doing life and five years for kidnapping, bank robbery and violation of the National Motor Vehicle Act. He had enough nerve to escape from another prison and organize a gang of bank robbers. But he lacked the gumption to serve out his time in Alcatraz.

A guard spotted him hunched over the railing in front of his third-tier cell peering down on the concrete floor below. The guard brought him to the hospital, explaining Wylie had "blown his top" and was acting strange.

"What's the idea?" I asked.

Wylie shrugged his shoulders in a gesture of hopelessness.

"I can't make my time. I may as well kill myself. I wanted to bump myself off by diving over that railing head first."

He was moved to a cell on the ground floor. Later he attempted to hang himself by tearing off a piece of his blanket. A guard discovered him before any damage was done. His cell was stripped of everything with which he might harm himself.

Ironically, among the would-be suicides were gangsters who had meted out death to others before their incarceration. Yet at Alcatraz, they hesitated to take their own lives.

"I got life and 50 years," one gangster explained. "The only thing that stops me is that I can't get up enough nerve to knock myself off."

Guard tower viewed from the upper roadway.

The scene resembled something from a Spanish Inquisition torture chamber. A single light bulb illuminated the cell. Shadows loomed grotesquely on the concrete wall, latticed by silhouetted bars. Guards surrounded a prisoner who was lying flat on his back. He scowled up at them defiantly.

I twirled a long rubber tube with a funnel attached and the deputy warden held a pitcher containing a white liquid. I jammed the long rubber tube into the prisoner's nostrils and shoved it in, further and further, until it almost disappeared. The deputy warden started pouring the liquid through the funnel. It was eggnog. The prisoner gagged and choked. His eyes watered. He paled. The eggnog gurgled down the tube, into the nostrils, the mouth, and the stomach.

"Four pints," I said.

"Make it five," the deputy warden commanded.

Tube feeding was an often-used disciplinary measure at Alcatraz, chiefly among hunger strikers. Certain prisoners rebelled at the harsh prison routine, went into tantrums and refused to eat. One force-fed meal and they usually changed their minds and decided to eat. They found the gagging horrible. There were some stubborn individuals who tolerated it for days.

Four pints of eggnog were the required daily amounts administered through the tube. So when the deputy warden ordered five pints, I knew it was ordered to bloat the prisoner and make him sick.

And then we hoped he would start eating. The fifth pint did just that. His prison garb started to bulge around his stomach. He had difficulty restraining the eggnog and writhed with nausea.

"I'll eat – I'll eat," he gasped, yanking the tube from his nose and retching.

The pitcher crashed to the floor, splattering the eggnog. This infuriated the deputy.

"Put the tube in again," he demanded.

I refused, maintaining that the pitcher had broken by accident. Then the deputy called for a tray of food. He placed it on the prisoner's lap and told him to eat if he knew what was good for him.

The prisoner, Lafayette Thomas, was caught damaging garments in the laundry and was placed in the dungeon. After spending nineteen days there, he was transferred to isolation. Then he began a hunger strike because he wanted two meals a day but was only getting one. Thomas was force fed for eight days before he finally capitulated.

Two methods of tube feeding were practiced at Alcatraz – nasal and mouth. Nasal was easier to perform. Mouth gave the most trouble because it gagged the patient, making him cough. Invariably, the patient bit on the tube. To thwart this, a wooden wedge was screwed into the prisoner's mouth.

A prisoner admitted defeat and vowed to be good after being fed so much liquid that his stomach inflated like a balloon and pushed out his coveralls. Such was the case with Phillip Dimanza, who went on a hunger strike after refusing to work. Throughout fourteen days of tube feeding, he acted as though it wasn't phasing him the slightest. In the midst of the feedings, he interrupted by singing, laughing, and joking.

After the tenth day, he enjoyed it and goaded us into feeding him more. He was actually trying on the hospital staff's nerves.

"Dimanza," I asked, "when are you going to cut out the nonsense and eat?"

"Never," he affirmed. "You'll have to feed me forever. I don't care. I have nothing to live for. As far as I'm concerned, I died years ago."

Following the fourteenth tube feeding, I decided either I would break Dimanza or he would break me.

"Dimanza," I warned, "I'm going to have a surprise for you tomorrow. You'll wish you never started this hunger strike business. When I get through, you'll eat."

Dimanza smiled.

The following noon, I arrived with seven pints of eggnog. Dimanza leaned back and took it. Then a pint of water was poured down the tube. This made one complete gallon of liquid. Dimanza's stomach looked like a balloon about to burst. Dimanza looked down at the bulge and paled.

"Doc," he gasped, "I .... I can't take any more .... I'm full up."

"Dimanza," I said, "if you think this is anything, I'm coming around tomorrow with twice as much!"

Dimanza swayed to and fro.

"Ohhhhhhh," he moaned, "I feel like a tire that's had way too much air shot into it."

Later he announced he would begin eating again. He couldn't stand the thought of another bout with the tube.

Then there was the case of Burton Phillips, the prisoner who assaulted the warden during the prison strike. After his recovery and discharge from the hospital, he was sentenced to nineteen days in solitary, and then placed in isolation. While in isolation, he cursed the food, refusing it. I asked why he wasn't eating.

"I'll tell you why I won't eat," he grumbled. "All I get is greasy stuff – soup with a lot of fat in it, and bread. I don't get any leafy vegetables. No greens at all. It isn't a balanced diet. I'm getting sick."

I spoke to the deputy warden about the food. It was decided that cereals would be given to prisoners in isolation three times a week. It took several days before the new cereal regime started and Phillips, thinking his complaints ignored, went on a hunger strike. It lasted one day. A pitcher of soup was brought to his cell and with it a nasal tube.

"Sit on the floor," a guard ordered.

"If you want your food this way, rather than eating it from a plate, it's all right with me," I commented.

"Start the party," Phillips scowled.

The tube going down wasn't a comfortable sensation. Phillips writhed. I held the funnel. A guard poured the soup. Phillips turned white and began to retch.

"Hold it down, Phillips," the guard warned. "If you heave it up we'll pour it right back down again."

Phillips regurgitated some of the soup. The guard caught the geyser-like spout and poured it down the tube again. This was too much for Phillips. Yanking the tube out, he gasped, "Okay, I'll eat – I'll eat."

Alcatraz had other effective disciplinary measures – like the rigid surveillance and tagging of prisoners.

Yes, they tagged prisoners at Alcatraz for infractions of prison rules, just as motorists are tagged for violations of the motor vehicle code. Only the prisoners called it "getting shot." Tags were carried in pad form in a guard's hip pocket. They were written on the slightest provocation, but mostly for insolence, fighting, and talking in the cellblock.

Talking in the cellblock was forbidden. If a prisoner was overheard gossiping with a pal in an adjoining cell, a guard immediately broke it up, whisked out his shot pad and jotted down the offending prisoner's name, number and violation with the precision of a motorcycle officer filling out a speeding ticket.

The prisoner was given the citation. A copy went to the deputy warden and the next day the prisoner appeared at "court call." It was held daily in the cellblock. Sitting as judge was the deputy warden. No gavel rested on the desk that was his bench. Instead a guard, gun held ready for instant action, paced above in the gun gallery.

The deputy warden studied the shot tags before him and engaged in verbal ping-pong with the prisoners confronting him. They were each given a chance to tell their story. Then the deputy warden weighed the evidence and ruled on each prisoner's guilt or innocence. If guilty, the prisoner was disciplined by demoting him to a lower grade.

Prisoners were graded at Alcatraz, just as though they were youngsters in school. There was first, second, and third grade. All new prisoners were classified as first grade. This meant they enjoyed meager privileges, such as the occasional movie, weekend recreation period, permission to write one letter a week, and the government-donated tobacco.

When a prisoner was reduced to second grade, his letter writing was limited to two letters a month. Should he be demoted to third grade, he was deprived of all privileges and was sentenced to the disciplinary cells – solitary confinement, isolation or the dungeon.

A more humane type of discipline was industrial good time. This put prisoners on their best behavior with a promise that, if they behaved, they would have days deducted from their prison sentence. This was an incentive to many.

James V. Bennett, director of the Bureau of Prisons, announced the following regulations effective January 1, 1938:

"A prisoner, to receive the industrial good time, must apply himself to the tasks assigned in a faithful, diligent, industrious, and orderly manner. No industrial good time will be allowed to any prisoner who refuses to do the work assigned to him by a foreman or custodial officer, who assaults or attempts to assault an officer, who escapes, attempts to escape, evades or hides out from a count, who willfully damages material, machinery, equipment, or other government property."

The industrial good time applied to prisoners working in the various workshops. It was accumulated at the rate of two days for each calendar month during the first year; four days for each calendar month during the second and subsequent years.

Prisoners of the small fry variety, who had only ten or fifteen years to serve, behaved to get industrial good time. But the former public enemies, serving fifty years or life, saw no incentive in it, well knowing only death would release them from the Rock.

It was these long-term prisoners that went on rampages, hunger strikes and other strikes. They were the ones who went to the disciplinary cells. These cells were dreaded because they meant being cut off from other prisoners.

Similarly, tobacco was not allowed prisoners in the disciplinary cells, although sometimes it was smuggled in. Prisoners in these cells were cooped up in utter silence, as though entombed alive.

It was the loneliness, the maddening silence, where time dragged and each second seemed an eternity that made good boys out of misbehaving prisoners. Most of them needed an audience to swagger before. Shunted into oblivion in a disciplinary cell, they were no longer headliners, entertaining their pals.

The dungeon was most feared. Perhaps the name dungeon was responsible – a name that conjured up visions of a dank, dark hole; rats scurrying about; sea water sloshing in ankle deep; prisoners bound to the wall by rusted irons; green slime on the walls. Dungeons, located under the cellblock, were pitch black. In the Army days, they were storerooms. Despite fantastic tales of released Alcatraz prisoners that men placed there were knee-deep in water, the dungeon cells were desert dry and totally bare. Lavatories were lacking; buckets were used instead. Prisoners contented themselves with lying on the concrete floor rolled up in a blanket. Solid steel doors sealed off the entrances. Guards handed water to the prisoner from the outside at intervals. It was indeed dismal.

Prisoners ordered to the dungeon shrieked in protest, groveled on the floor and insisted they would behave, if only they weren't sent there.

The isolation and solitary cells were located on the side of the cellhouse. Isolation cells had not been remodeled since the Army days. They had all the conveniences of a typical cell. But the men were restricted to them twenty-four hours daily, with no privileges and received only two meals a day.

Isolation was called "Siberia." The isolation cells were so situated that the prisoner faced a concrete wall. Some cells, however, had barred window openings with a sweeping view of San Francisco Bay.

Solitary confinement – or the hole – was more severe. Prisoners in solitary were isolated in semi-darkness. There were ten such cells. In some cells, all light was blotted out by wooden storm doors placed over the steel-barred doors. In other cells, the metal barred doors were filled in with cement to shut out the light. At the bottom of these doors was a small area, heavily screened for ventilation, through which food was pushed.

Solitary cells had no lights, no beds – only a toilet and washbasin. The men in solitary were issued one or two blankets. They rolled themselves in the blankets and slept on the floor. A man was placed in solitary only nineteen days in succession, with one meal every three days and bread in between. After nineteen days, he was removed. But he could be sent back again the next day for another nineteen days.

Maximum security was another example of enforcing discipline. There was the continual banging of steel doors – to the right, left, ahead, and behind the prisoners. Ominous tear gas and nauseating gas containers hung like silver chandeliers on the ceilings. Weapons – such as submachine guns, revolvers, automatic rifles, and gas billys – were carried by the guards.

Constant shakedowns to detect concealed weapons or contraband also enforced maximum security. Then there was the guard's incessant target practice. This drilled into the prisoner's minds the futility of making a break, of how they would be stopped with a hail of sharpshooter bullets.

"Shakedown!"

A formula for some sort of explosive, carefully written on a bit of paper, was found in the cell of Silent Jim Ryan, one-time member of the Touhy Gang. "Potassium nitrate, 12 parts; sulfur 2 parts; carbon 2 parts."

Immediately Alcatraz "peet men" (safe crackers) who knew explosive mixtures were put under surveillance. Then began the rigorous shakedown. Shakedown was a methodical, relentless search in which cells and workshops were probed for weapons, razor blades, narcotics, or ingredients to make explosives.

Guards poured into the cells, yanked aside blankets, groped with nimble fingers through the bedclothes and fluttered the leaves of books, hoping something concealed might drop out. They peered into cracks, shelves, washbasins, lavatories and light bulbs. A similar microscopic examination occurred in the workshops. Machinery was taken apart and examined; tools and supplies were checked and rechecked.

Guards found a large piece of sulfur concealed in the blacksmith shop. And, because Silent Jim worked as an orderly in the hospital where he could fill such a formula, the hospital was also checked. Officials, ever on the alert, suspected some sort of large-scale escape plot – with the possibility of gunpowder being manufactured clandestinely by the prisoners.

Shakedowns of individual prisoners occurred many times each day, as they went to and from work, and in and out of the cellblock. Two electric metal detectors, or "snitches," were passed in the long trek from the work area to the cellblock. A guard stood on duty by the snitch. This device, referred to as a "hot dog stand" by the prisoners, had a fine green line on a glass screen, like a carpenter's leveling plumb. When metal passed through the snitch, the fine green line disappeared and was replaced by a red light. Simultaneously, a loud buzzing was heard.

There were three snitches on Alcatraz. One at the dock, through which everyone entering or leaving Alcatraz passed; one at the entrance to the Administration Building; and one at the cellblock entrance.

Everything brought to Alcatraz was taken apart and thoroughly examined. This applied to food, groceries and meats coming into the prison. Kegs of flour, sugar and other loose, powdered products were sifted to be sure that no contraband or weapons were smuggled in.

The heart of Alcatraz was the Armory. This room was never, at any time, and no matter what the circumstances, unoccupied. It was the controlling unit and was in constant contact with all parts of Alcatraz. Guards called into the Armory every half-hour for a checkup. A small war could be waged with the weapons stored there.

Before reporting on duty, guards obtained their weapons from the Armory. They were handed out through a small door and returned in the same manner.

Bulletproof glass and tool-proof steel made Alcatraz almost like a fortress. The interior of the buildings resembled garrisons. Bulletproof glass was everywhere.

There were five combinations of steel doors and locks to enter the prison through the Administration Building. Between the main gate and cellhouse gate were two large gas cartridges that resembled sleek airplane bombs. The guard on duty in the Armory electrically controlled them. Should anyone storm the cellhouse gate, the Armory guard could, by a touch of the finger, let loose the gas bombs.

The guard patrolling the catwalk outside the mess hall electrically controlled the gas cartridges suspended from the mess hall ceiling. There were electrical indicators in the Armory to detect tampering.

Maximum security was reflected even in the cellhouse. The individual cells were made of concrete. They were approximately four feet wide and eight and a half feet long. The entrance door was made of tool-proof steel bars. On one side of the cell, suspended from the wall by chains, was a metal bed with interwoven wide metal bands for a spring.

Suspended from the middle of the other wall was a small iron folding table. The bed was used as a chair when the table was lowered. At the back wall, behind the bed, was the toilet. Beside it was a small washbasin with cold water only. High up on the rear wall was a shelf for personal belongings. Each cell was a compact one-room apartment.

The cellblocks contained rows of cells. At the end of each row was a large steel box. When open, it displayed several handles and levers. By manipulating these levers, one or all of the cells opened or closed.

An even, comfortable temperature was maintained in the cellhouse using steam heat. Each cell had an opening for ventilation near the floor. The prisoners relished some cells as "choice sites." Those near the upper west side of the cellhouse faced the Golden Gate and the new bridge that spanned it. Here prisoners could watch the ships inching their way in and out of San Francisco Bay and enjoy the sunsets, with their oil painting-like magnificence.

Gun catwalks, for guards with rifles, were on both sides of the cellhouse. The catwalks were balconies, three to four feet wide, latticed with steel. A guard was present in each catwalk day and night. Guards bearing rifles were confined to the towers, walls and catwalks. The guards who mixed with the prisoners were equipped only with gas billys. This prevented the prisoners from getting a firearm and possibly overpowering a guard. Guards on the gun galleries in the cellblock were weighted down with automatic rifles, gas guns, heavy cartridge belts and huge gas cartridges that circled their waists.

From each gun gallery, a powerful floodlight was directed on the large middle aisle of the cellhouse. Because it was lit twenty-four hours a day, the prisoners called it "Broadway."

At the rear of the cellhouse was the entrance to the yard. A twenty-foot high concrete wall surrounded the yard itself, on top of which was the catwalk patrolled by guards. In the middle of the yard wall was a solid steel door. It was the entrance to the workshop area.

A long stretch of ground led to the workshops. On their way to the workshops, the prisoners had a grim reminder. To the right of them was the target range frequented throughout the day by groups of guards. Tall fences and hedges of barbed wire, making the work area resemble some tremendous cage, hemmed in the many workshops and buildings. Above was a system of towers and catwalks.

Two electrically controlled gates guarded the entrance to the work area for automobiles and trucks. A guard in the tower above maneuvered these gates. The tower guard controlled the gate to the incinerator, through which the garbage trucks passed. He lowered the key to the men below on a long string.

Maximum security was further assured when the government named James J. Johnston as warden. He previously served in a similar capacity at California's Folsom and San Quentin penitentiaries. He won national recognition for helping to end a twenty-four hour Thanksgiving Day riot at Folsom prison in 1927.

Science also played its part in maximum security. Besides the electric snitches, Alcatraz was in constant radio communication with the Coast Guard station at San Francisco. Regular signals were sent from Alcatraz to the Coast Guard officials. If these signals failed to come in, gray Coast Guard boats would immediately steam to Alcatraz and investigate. Thus, should the prisoners gain control of the Rock, they would fight the Coast Guard.

A rigorous check of visitors provided further maximum security. All employees and residents of Alcatraz were furnished with identification cards. They were presented whenever requested. Employees expecting visitors were responsible for them during their brief stay.

Alcatraz thus took on the aspects of some Forbidden City. It was practically impossible for the curious to enter this Lhassa, even in disguise. The regulations were designed to prevent tourists, curiosity seekers, sightseeing groups, or chance acquaintances from visiting. But more so, the rigid rules sought to prevent the prisoner's former associates from visiting them and plotting escape.

The mysteriousness attached to Alcatraz, through rigid government censorship, was yet another effective disciplinary tool. People seldom read about Alcatraz because newspapers were unable to get any information. Either the Department of Justice or the warden gave the only news that did eke out. And they had to be momentous stories – an escape or the warden being attacked – before the government sanctioned their release.

"No comment" was usually Warden Johnston's terse reply whenever a reporter phoned to check on something.

"The prisoners in Alcatraz are out of the limelight. We intend to keep them out of the limelight," he explained.

When news of Al Capone's mental collapse leaked out of Alcatraz, Warden Johnston refused to comment.

RECREATION AND PRIVILEGES

Each night the riders of the purple sage went galloping through Alcatraz. And in fancy the gray-clad prisoners went with them. Lying in his cot, a Western thriller clutched in his hands, the average prisoner was so absorbed that he was oblivious to the moaning foghorns, the sloshing waves, and the hobnailed boots clomping through the cellblock.

If ever there was a justifiable need for escape literature, it was on Alcatraz. Wearied from long hours in the prison workshop, unable to converse with fellow prisoners, and chafed at being confined in a single cell, the prisoner flipped open a battered, dog-eared Western novel from the Alcatraz library. Poof! He was jogging under the light of the western stars, squatting around a campfire with the boys of the old Bar X, engaging in smoky-gun battles, and winning the heroine. Then the lights-out signal clanged and he was plunged back into drab reality.

Reading was the chief recreation in Alcatraz. Westerns were the most favored with travel books the next favored. Books were borrowed from the prison library, which incidentally added Dale Carnegie's *How To Win Friends and Influence People*. Newspapers and newspaper clippings were forbidden. Prison officials approved 74 magazines. Some titles were *Atlantic Monthly, Better Homes and Gardens, B'Nai Brith, Christian Science Sentinel, Collier's, Cosmopolitan, Etude, Field and Stream, Fortune, National Geographic, Nature,*

Newsweek, New Yorker, Outdoor Life, Popular Mechanics, Saturday Evening Post, Trailer Travel, Turkey World, Writers Digest, and *Yachting.* The popular pulp detective thrillers and slick true detective magazines were conspicuously missing. Books and magazines were received directly from the publishers, according to Alcatraz rules. This prevented smuggling hidden messages or narcotics in the printed matter. Still, as an added precaution, the clean, unturned pages were carefully scrutinized in the prison office. There was another reason for this inspection – the Department of Justice kept all criminal activities of the outside world from the prisoners.

Certain articles were allowed to pass through uncensored for their psychological effect. These included "crime doesn't pay" articles and stories of G-men (Federal Bureau of Investigation agents) wiping out gangs. Still, despite the clip out system and the absence of newspapers and radios, news did reach the prisoners. The morning following an attempted escape at Folsom prison, in which the warden was fatally stabbed, one prisoner asked me if the warden was dead.

Certain prisoners were allowed to work in the civilian employee's homes, repairing and painting. They often snatched hasty glances at a newspaper.

The library, located in the cellhouse, contained many volumes of fiction, non-fiction and educational works. A list of available books was given to each new prisoner. They obtained reading matter by writing the name of the book on a request slip. A prisoner could borrow as many books as he desired, unless his privileges were forfeited for some infraction of prison rules.

In Alcatraz, where privileges were minimal, even a matter-of-fact thing like letter writing was considered a cherished rite, a break from the monotonous routine. Prisoners were allowed to write one letter a week.

As a prisoner mechanically performed his shop task, he probably mused on just what witticisms, just what impassioned longings he would pen. On the evening of the letter writing "rite," the prisoner took paper and pencil, and proceeded to pour out his loneliness to a dear one or friend.

No inspired Zola or Dickens ever wrote as sincerely as an Alcatraz prisoner. Eyebrows were knit as he stared down at the spaced paper, making penciled loops and scrawls and dots. He was absorbed. It was communion, communion with someone who cared. It might be a wife or child or mother. Their faces loomed up before the writer – kind, understanding, sympathetic.

No longer was the prisoner a number, a being who rose, dressed, ate, worked, and rested at a prescribed time. Pencil clutched in his hand, he was a man, capable of love and passion, and could say what he pleased. Condemned though he was to the Rock, and subjected to the harsh discipline, these words on paper were one of the few contacts he had with the civilized world.

As one prisoner explained,

"It's just like I was talking to Molly. I imagined we were in our apartment, with the fire crackling in the fireplace, and all comfortable and cozy-like, and me resting easy like and comfortable on the overstuffed Chesterfield. And maybe there's a scotch 'n soda handy nearby on the side table with the sportin' page right alongside, where Molly always put it, considerate-like."

"And I've got my shoes off, and am wrigglin' my toes in my socks, real comfortable. And Molly and me start gabbin.' Nothing wise-cracky or flip. No clownin.' Just – well – sort of talkin' philosophical-like. Quiet-like, like man and wife usually talk. About our kid, and how we're goin' to send him to college and give him the chances we never had, about life and how cockeyed it is."

"And then I come to the last line on the paper and have to close with the usual 'Your ever lovin' husband' and it's then that I come to with a jolt."

His letter to Molly first went to the Island's mail censor. The prisoner knew this. But sentimental softie that he was, he tenderly caressed the letter, pressed it to his lips, and fondled it before placing it in the plain brown envelope.

A mail censor eyed all incoming and outgoing letters, transcribing them into typewritten form. The prisoner's pitiful, scrawled outpourings to his Molly became cold and mechanical – words clicked off by the prison censor's typewriter. A letter from Molly was also typewritten before being given to the prisoner. The neat, carefully spaced and punctuated typewritten words made the letter as impersonal as a direct mail advertisement. The exact wording of all incoming and outgoing letters was never used. Certain phrases and peculiar wordings were deleted because they might be part of a code or might convey some secret message. Letters were also transcribed and typed to prevent narcotics from entering the prison. Glue used to seal an envelope might contain morphine. The stationery on an incoming letter might be saturated with other drugs. Persons to whom an Alcatraz prisoner might write were carefully scrutinized. Prisoners were not allowed to communicate with gangsters or people with questionable reputations. Letters could only be written to relatives and friends of good character.

After the mail censor typed an incoming letter, he placed it in a brown envelope with the prisoner's number on it and gave it to the cellhouse guard. The guard delivered the letters following the night lock up. The prisoners eagerly awaited his appearance. In his wake he left smiles from those who received mail, grimaces of disappointment from the others.

Prisoners were allowed to receive as many letters as were sent to them. When privileges were forfeited for violating prison rules, all letters were withheld and saved until such privileges were restored.

Another cherished event was recess time. Prisoners were allowed outside for several hours on Saturday and Sunday afternoons. After being cooped up all week, they came pouring into the yard like gleeful school youngsters released for a brief respite of play. It was here that they became carefree and vented their pent-up emotions in laughter, talk, and exercise.

They congregated in groups and factions. Some preferred to be alone. But most of them laughed and joked and took playful jabbing pokes at each other. Some paired up and walked around and around the yard for exercise. Others sat on the stone steps near the entrance and chatted or played checkers and chess. Many stripped to the waist and sat on the ground, sunbathing.

Baseball, handball and horseshoe tossing were the most popular sports. Tossing a horseshoe or running after low bunts or hopping about bouncing a ball against the side of a court was rather drab stuff compared to the other forms of recreation most of the prisoners once had.

Yet now they ran about and cavorted like over zealous children in a playground. Baseball was the most interesting sport available. They whooped and yelled when a good hit was made or booed loudly on a miss. A system of teams and leagues was devised and, although a hard indoor baseball was used, it was the fastest game to watch. Here was an outlet for their pent-up emotions. They played as avidly as any big league team out to win the pennant.

They played so hard that accidents were quite common. One prisoner whammed out a hit and started sprinting to first base. A fielder leaped high in the air, snagged the ball and heaved it with express-train speed to the first baseman. In a frantic effort to beat the ball, the batter dove for the base headfirst. He beat the ball by a split second. And even though he fractured his leg and was unable to get up, a triumphant grin spread across his face when he learned he was safe. He was confined to the hospital for eight weeks. Handball enthusiasts were equally reckless. The handball court adjoined the horseshoe stakes. In their frenzy to retrieve a fleeting ball and make one desperate effort to send it thudding against the court, many players leaped out into the horseshoe pitching area, unmindful of the metal shoes that came whizzing through the air. And if they did get "conked" by a shoe, they didn't mind. Numerous windows were broken by the ballplayer's terrific hits. Each time a ball smashed into a window, the entire yard greeted the crash-tinkle with jubilant cries. Because of the damage, screening was placed across the windows. Many prisoners watched eagerly, even though they had no desire for the knock-down-and-drag-out ball playing. The hospital patients dragged themselves to the windows and watched every game.

There wasn't much of a sick line on Saturday and Sunday. Even though some had the sniffles or a headache or indigestion, they didn't want to be confined to the hospital because of illness. They took their chances and went out for a little air and freedom.

During these treasured hours, the prisoners ran and jumped and shouted and cursed and talked and laughed and got all sweaty and tired from exhilarating athletic competition. They forgot the clanging gongs that ordered them about, the monotony of the workshops, and the long tiresome hours at night in their cells. They felt the blood surging through their veins, felt their bodies respond to their wills as they cavorted in the yard. For the time being, they were neither men entombed nor listless, silent shells of men.

The yard was not complete freedom. For above them, ominous and aloof, were the tower guards. They walked to and fro, to and fro – like restless beasts of prey. Their repeating automatic rifles were held ready to "pour it on" should any emergency arise. The instructions on Alcatraz were "shoot to kill if necessary." And the gray-clad prisoners below were ever mindful that one misstep and a bullet would stop them.

"Going to the movies" was another rare treat.

The world of make believe came to Alcatraz in tin film containers. Movies were restricted to only seven or eight a year. Every prisoner looked forward to them as eagerly as a visit from a loved one. Men in isolation and solitary confinement, who refused to eat or work, softened when word was whispered that there was going to be a movie. Their rebellious scowls disappeared. They became humble, expressing a burning desire to return to work. And all this so they could see a movie.

Movies were shown following the noon meal on a holiday. Prisoners were neatly dressed in their holiday blue uniforms. A festive air permeated the cellblock. Everyone was expectant. You've seen youngsters in your neighborhood that have wheedled money from their parents for a matinee and were just bursting with expectancy. Well, the Alcatraz prisoners were equally enthusiastic.

"What're we gonna see?" was the question of the day and it was on every lip.

"I hope it ain't no Shirley Temple or Bobby Breen picture again," some said fervently.

"Boy, I hope it's Joe E. Brown or Laurel and Hardy."

No parent teacher's group, making an approved list of what pictures youngsters ought to see and ought not, ever chose films as rigidly as they did at Alcatraz. Movies dealing with crime or gangsters were forbidden. So were the passionate romance type movies. This narrowed the list to musicals, cartoons, comedies, biographies and historical sagas. Joe E. Brown, Laurel and Hardy, Popeye, Shirley Temple, and Bobby Breen were considered safe.

The prisoners hurried through the noon meal and awaited the bell that signaled movie time. When it rang, they started for the small theater above the Administration Room. Each prisoner was shaken down before leaving the cellhouse. The shakedown routine was done with zip and a flourish now. They were in a hurry and cooperated.

Prison officials ordered the shakedown before the movie as a precaution. They knew the danger of crowding cooped-up prisoners into a tiny, dark auditorium. Hatred between two men – or certain cliques – might be climaxed during the movie with a knife stealthily slipped out of a sleeve and thrust into the back of the man ahead. For this reason, many prisons prohibited movies.

When the shakedown failed to unearth any weapons, the prisoners filed into the small theater. Soon the folding chairs were occupied and those who followed stood along the sides. Their behavior was excellent. No loud talk. No rowdy cheers. No playful jabs. They realized only too well that should an outbreak or disturbance of any kind occur, they would be forbidden to attend future movies.

The lights dimmed. The screen blazed with light as the cartoon *Popeye* appeared. Contented "ahhhhhh's" swept through the theater, followed by anticipated chuckles. Bulgy-muscled Popeye started cavorting about. Gales of laughter greeted his every antic. When the inevitable climax came, in which Popeye hauled out a can of spinach, ate it, and started annihilating his rival to the tune of *Stars and Stripes Forever*, the prisoners laughed hysterically.

Laughter on the Rock! It sounded incredible at first. Gleeful howls, hearty guffaws, yelps of pleased delight, all coming from these men who on the morrow would be sitting tight-lipped and surly in their cells. Then *The End* flashed and the men sat back, smiles wreathing their faces, waiting for the feature film. They were content.

Fortunately, the picture that day was *Way Out West* with Laurel and Hardy. Had it been one starring any of the current juvenile favorites, it would be greeted with sighs of disappointment. The prisoners wanted to laugh. It was something they did so seldom. And watching the too-cute antics of some youngster with a cherubic face bored them.

"I guess it's because when we were kids we were holy terrors," one prisoner explained.

The picture unfolded and with it continued gales of laughter. They absorbed every bit of tomfoolery and eyed every gag and wisecrack.

After the movie, the prisoners continually evoked howls of laughter from each other by aping one of the outstanding gags in the picture. It consisted of Stan Laurel bending back his thumb, which then started blazing like a cigarette lighter. For days, the prisoners went about bending their thumbs, and making believe it had suddenly burst into flame.

Prisoner Thomas made a window repair in my father's home while Guard Rose observed him.

The Dude always loathed alarm clocks. He couldn't even stand the most delicate ones that wheedled and cajoled one into getting up. He invariably slept way past noon. One of his aides would slip into the swank pale orchid bedroom and gently hoist the Venetian blinds, letting in the afternoon sun. He blinked, opened his eyes, yawned contentedly, stripped off his pale orchid pajamas and climbed lazily out of bed.

[At Alcatraz, the 6:30 a.m. rousing gong bolted the Dude awake. Its incessant clang-a-lang-a-lang was heard over the entire Island. He leaped out of his iron cot, shivering. Wisps of clammy fog swirled through his cell. He hastily donned his prison coveralls, jamming them up over his pajamas – long, ankle-length woolen drawers.]

The Dude luxuriated in a scented tub, and then massaged himself dry with a huge monogrammed towel. He put on his pale orchid silk shorts, slicked back his hair, and swathed himself in a loud, expensive dressing robe. He lolled about smoking innumerable cigarettes, dribbling ash over the floor and flipping aside the butts as he read the sports page.

[Once the Dude donned his gray uniform, he bustled about cleaning his cell. Regulations decreed that on arising a prisoner must make his bed, wipe off the bars of his cell, place his belongings on a shelf, sweep the cell, and put the refuse just outside the bars. Cigarette butts and ashes, burnt matches and pipe cleanings were placed in the toilet bowl and flushed. His table and seat were folded against the wall.]

The Dude donned his double-breasted gray suit, with the pale orchid shirt and tie to match. He plopped himself down to a spacious table, furbished with snowy linen, gleaming silverware, and rainbow-hued flowers.

[The second morning gong rang at 6:50 a.m. The Dude was ready for breakfast, his cell immaculate. He stood facing the door ready for the checkup count. A whistle sounded. Cell doors clanged open and disgorged their occupants. Prisoners marched in single file to the mess hall.]

The Dude first guzzled a glass of chilled pineapple juice in those pre-Alcatraz days. He delved into iced melon shipped from California and proceeded to wolf a huge stack of hotcakes and little sausages, all swimming in butter and maple syrup. Occasionally he sipped hot black coffee, his favorite expensive brand. He belched heartily and called for seconds.

[At Alcatraz, it was the usual breakfast of hot or cold cereal. The Dude ate hurriedly. The rules said that not more than twenty minutes were allowed for eating. He stared at the scrubbed table before him and sighed, remembering the snowy linen.]

Thus began a typical day for the Dude and the other prisoners. The design for living on Alcatraz was the mimeographed sheet of paper containing the rules and regulations. Most new prisoners were amazed at the long hours of work and the factory-like precision.

Work started at 7:30 a.m. The prisoners were permitted one smoke in the yard before beginning their work. They lounged about, puffed cigarettes made of the government-furnished tobacco and talked listlessly. If it had been a foggy night, they damned the Alcatraz symphony – the Rock's blatant foghorn. It kept them awake with its incessant moaning.

Then a guard blew his whistle. It was the signal for attention. Smoking and talking ceased. Cigarette butts were ground into the earth with heavy prison shoes. Work details lined up and marched in single file to the various prison workshops.

At 9:30 a.m., the prisoners were given an eight-minute rest period. They were allowed to smoke or go to the washroom, one at a time. The rules decreed that prisoners must remain as near their work as possible. At no time were they permitted to loiter in shops other than where they were assigned to work.

The huge workshop area was on the far side of the Island beyond the prison and the yard. Tower guards had a sweeping view of the entire area, the most heavily guarded in the entire prison.

On foggy days, when the possibility of escape was great, the prisoners were not allowed in the work area. They were herded into the yard, where they paraded about, waiting for the mist to lift. On regular recreation days, they played games in the yard and talked. But on workdays, while waiting for the fog to dissipate, they could only walk to and fro, an endless activity that took them nowhere.

Civilians were employed to supervise the various industrial shops. They were experienced men who knew, in every detail, the workmanship necessary for the manufacture of the articles in their shops. There was no antagonism between the supervisors and the prisoners. Supervisors were not guards and did not wear uniforms. Nor did they goad the prisoners on to faster activity. The prisoners listened to them and obeyed their instructions. Sometimes words arose between a supervisor and a prisoner, whereupon a guard on duty bluntly informed the prisoner to do as he was told.

There were 46 different jobs in the various workshops. Work was divided into two groups: (1) work necessary for the immediate maintenance of the Island and the prisoners, and (2) industries that produced materials for outside use.

One of the larger shops was the tailor shop. It hummed with activity. With its electrically operated machines arranged in rows, the shop was reminiscent of a garment factory. About thirty-eight prisoners were kept busy there. Each sat behind his machine, intently eyeing the work before him, carefully piecing the patterns together. The civilian shop foreman passed among the prison-workers, ever present to aid them. Here they manufactured the dark suits that eventually were given to prisoners when they were discharged from various prisons. Some of the clothing was sold to the Veteran's Bureau, which furnished suits to disabled war veterans.

Odds and ends of cloth littered the floor. The many dark suits already completed hung at the entrance to the shop. The clatter of the machines was incessant. Long, sharp scissors needed to cut the cloth were obtained by asking a guard. These were carefully tracked, the officials being ever mindful of the havoc they might cause should one be smuggled back into the cellblock.

The largest and most active industry was the laundry. It kept some ninety prisoners busy. Vast as a big city commercial laundry and similarly equipped with machinery and mechanics, this shop did the laundry for many government agencies – Army transports arriving in San Francisco Bay, nearby Army fortification posts, Angel Island (the U.S. Immigration Depot), and Alcatraz. The swishing and whirring of the huge washing machines and the din of the mangles was heard daily.

The laundry occupied two floors. An elevator – operated by a prisoner – and an outside staircase connected the two levels. When the bundles of dirty laundry arrived, they were pawed over and sorted by ten prisoners who worked in the distributing department. Six markers put identification marks on the various pieces, so that they were returned to the rightful owners. Then the sorted, marked laundry was sent to the washers. Fourteen men manipulated these revolving, sudsy machines. They crammed them full with laundry and made sure that the clothes, sheets and tablecloths were clean. Then they took out the soggy and dripping laundry and relayed it to the prisoners at the mangles.

Twenty-two prisoners were at the mangles, feeding through bed sheets, towels and other flat work. This was a preferred job because the machine was simple to run and didn't require any great physical activity. A prisoner fed the laundry into the mangle and a fellow-prisoner helped guide it out.

The largest department in the laundry was the ironing room, where thirty prisoners labored. Workers greeted the arrival of an Army transport – and its thousands of soiled handkerchiefs, shirts and underwear – with oaths of disgust. They were literally snowed under with ironing.

Prisoners took time out from their work for a bit of horseplay. Pranks practiced in the Alcatraz laundry made the heavy transport work bearable, one prisoner confided. They deliberately tore and ruined the laundry but ironed, folded, and wrapped it neatly. Often, it wasn't until days later that the owner of the laundry detected the prank. Any inhabitant on the Island who was disliked by the prisoners soon learned that it was cheaper to have his laundry done in San Francisco – and pay for it – than to have it done free on Alcatraz – and ruined.

There was the case of a prison official that purchased six new shirts and sent them to the laundry before wearing them. He never got them back. Because of some hostile feeling toward him, the shirts found their way to the incinerator and were burned.

The shirts of another official were returned snowy white, ironed and folded. When he went to put one on, he started pulling out the pins that held it in place. He blinked in amazement as he extracted pin after pin – oodles of them. The shirt resembled a porcupine. He counted 225 pins before he was through!

In another instance, an Alcatraz official unfolded his just-back-from-the-laundry shirt and was amazed to find that the sleeves were cut off at the shoulder and neatly folded in place there again. And one shirt was redesigned when the fringe of a curtain was cut off and sewn onto its shirttail!

One of these pranks was played on me when I first came to Alcatraz. Each of six shirts I planned to wear on the Island had tabs attached to the collars. Each week, when the finished laundry was delivered, I found that one tab was missing. It had been pulled out. From then on, one tab was removed from every shirt, until all the tabs were yanked off.

With the laundry handled by so many men – markers, sorters, washers, and ironers – it was difficult to find the culprit. Numerous prisoners were placed in solitary confinement for mishandling laundry.

It was strange that the laundry housed the Alcatraz undercover publishing house. Should any prisoner ever write a poem lampooning the G-men or Alcatraz officials, it made its appearance in "book" form – pasted on the folded cardboard used in shirts. This is how they immortalized Theodore Cole and Ralph Roe, the escaped Alcatraz prisoners. A poem, *Gone with the Tide*, was distributed in this manner. *Gone With The Tide by Poor Old Johnston* (Warden Johnston) was emblazoned on the cover. (This poem appears in the chapter *Escape*.)

The shoe workshop employed three shoe repairers. A towering heap of shoes lay beside them – the thick prisoner type and the more delicate-appearing ones of the civilian population. Deftly, they removed old soles, reamed the shoe to prepare a sewing edge, and had a new sole on in no time.

In the blacksmith workshop, six prisoners forged chains to bind themselves. They heated and hammered metal into whatever form was needed, but mostly they constructed and repaired barriers – or bars – for themselves and the other prisoners.

The mat shop offered employment for the prisoner not gifted in things mechanical, or who had no aptitude for the usual shop work. Twenty-six men worked in the mat shop to produce rubber mats for the Navy's battleships. Worn, frayed or punctured tires were brought to Alcatraz and dumped on the dock. A prisoner cut each tire in half. This was done with a wooden sawhorse that had a heavy, sharp knife embedded in it – blade upward.

The prisoner straddled the sawhorse. Then he took each tire, raised it above his head and slammed it down over the knife. He pulled the tire toward him. The blade cleaved the tire in two.

Tires ripped open in this manner were piled 15 feet high on an open truck and slowly driven to the mat shop. The tires were then cut into easier-to-handle forms. A machine punched segments out, and these were sewn together by hand, making the finished mat.

Genuine craftsmanship flourished in the model workshop, which produced furniture, ashtrays, and lamps. The eight prisoners on duty there were among the few at Alcatraz who enjoyed their work and took pride in it. They had the finest electrical equipment to work with. The creative urge surged within them, in contrast to the prisoners who methodically plodded along in the laundry or mat shop, doing drab, routine work. These woodworkers regarded their work as the most interesting on the Island. They enjoyed the clean odor of fresh lumber, the whining of saws, and the scrunch of planes as they attacked a plank. They gleaned satisfaction from seeing a bit of lumber materialize into a floor lamp. It was a diversion that kept them from thinking of the harsh routine and the constant monotony.

Alcatraz was a self-sufficient community. Prisoner-carpenters, plumbers, glaziers, electricians, and road crews made repairs to its infrastructure.

Three prisoners comprised the carpenter shop. Their work didn't require the care or craftsmanship needed for the articles made in the model shop. These work-a-day carpenters repaired woodwork and built new structures. One of their achievements was a well-constructed indoor handball court.

The clean-up crew consisted of four men. They started work in the morning tidying up the Administration Building offices. Then they went outside, sweeping down the roadway, tending the shrubbery, trimming the flowers, watering the gardens, mowing the lawns, and removing dead branches from the trees. These men prided themselves on their work and they got outdoors. But the all-seeing eyes of the tower guards always watched them.

Three men worked as librarians, keeping the books in order and distributing the books to the prisoners.

There were thirteen cellhouse orderlies who kept it immaculate. They polished the cement floors by pushing around a bit of old blanket with a broom. At regular intervals, they waxed the cell floors with hand cloths or washed them with shaggy mops.

The prisoners almost worked an eight-hour day. As they trudged to their cells late in the afternoon, Alcatraz resembled a factory.

Following was the "design for living," the daily prisoner routine:

6:30 a.m.	Awake and clean cells.
6:50 a.m.	Morning checkup count.
7:00 a.m.	March to breakfast.
7:20 a.m.	Finish eating.
7:30 a.m.	Work begins.
9:30 a.m.	Rest period.
9:38 a.m.	Work resumes.
11:15 a.m.	Stop work.
11:40 a.m.	Dinner.
12:00 p.m.	Sick call at prison hospital. Interviews with warden, mail clerk, and Chaplain.
12:30 p.m.	March into yard, line up for work details.
12:40 p.m.	Work begins.
2:30 p.m.	Rest period.

2:38 p.m.	Work resumes.
4:10 p.m.	Stop work and return to cells.
4:25 p.m.	March into mess hall for supper.
4:45 p.m.	Return to cell for the night.
4:50 p.m.	Final lockup.
9:30 p.m.	Lights out.

Headline from the San Francisco Examiner.

Strike

The last rays of the setting sun dawdled lingeringly on Alcatraz, blurring its shimmering outlines and causing the Rock to resemble the Riviera – its turreted villas dropping tier upon tier to the blue water below. Ferry commuters that evening of September 1937 looked up from their newspapers and gazed at the stark security of a steel and concrete structure.

Despite its outward appearance of peace and stolidity, the Rock was in a state of siege. As though it were a factory beset by labor difficulties, Alcatraz was on strike. Unknown to the outside world, all routine had ceased. Bustling shops were silent and deserted. Prisoners languished in the cellblock – soon be transformed into a human zoo by the booing and shrieking from 300 throats.

The strike was called to protest the rigorous discipline and maddening monotony. Strikes broke out on the Rock about every fourteen months. New prisoners transferred from other institutions usually took the initiative. Old timers knew the futility of rebellion but joined in with the "fish" – newcomers – welcoming the strike as a break in the deadly routine.

Prisoners worked at their assigned shop tasks the morning of the strike. Everywhere there was an air of tense expectancy. Everyone on the Rock knew it was going to happen. The prisoners were planning for weeks – with whispered conversations in the workshops and during recreation periods. Stool pigeons tipped off the officials.

Even Alcatraz had stool pigeons. They received no rewards – no privileges, no words of appreciation, not even a smile of approval. The ecstasy of knowing and blabbing the news to an official was reward enough for a "stoolie." His was the same urge that motivated kindergarten urchins to tell the teacher that so-and-so was doing something wrong. It was the urge to ingratiate himself with someone in authority.

In anticipation of the strike, the guards were doubled on the ramparts. Submachine guns were distributed. Guards watched closely for anything that might be a signal. They watched lips, too, for speech was forbidden most of the day. But even the most alert guard could not catch words grunted out through lips that did not move.

"Twelve-thirty's the time. We'll show them."

"Lunch, then lock up. After that we don't budge."

During lunch, guns were pointed at the gray backs hunched over the long tables. Banging a tin coffee mug on tables like these had started many revolts in other prisons. But Alcatraz prisoners were smart; they knew the danger of bullets ricocheting against the concrete walls of the mess hall.

After lunch, the gray lines shuffled back to the cellblock for the customary brief after-lunch rest period. The parade was orderly. The guards relaxed. Maybe it wasn't going to happen after all. Maybe the "stoolies" were wrong.

The work whistle shrilled, ending the rest period. Cell doors clanged open. Twenty-six prisoners sprawled on their cots and refused to move. The strike was on!

Prison officials moved among them, prodding, questioning – trying to unearth the ringleaders. Those suspected of instigating the rebellion were hustled to solitary, the rest to isolation.

And then the first blow of violence struck. At 5 p.m. Alex Thomas was being escorted to isolation by three guards. Indignant at their prodding, Thomas smashed his fist into a guard's face, blackening his eye. Before the others could fling themselves on him, Thomas' fists lashed out again. Another guard was caught on the jaw. Thomas was jumped. In the ensuing scuffle, his nose was bashed. Kicking and bleeding, he was carried to isolation and stripped. Blankets were removed.

Night fell on the seething silence of the Rock. Nervously, the prisoners waited for someone to start something, anything. Wasn't that why they pulled the strike? Then one cut loose with a sea lion's roar.

"C'mon, wad'r we waiting for!"

A storm of yelling, cursing, and banging on the bars began. It raged and swept through the cellblock. Prisoners shouted foul oaths at the guards who ordered silence. They banged any and all moveable objects against bars and walls. They screamed and laughed, brayed and cackled, booed and cheered, barked and howled, hissed and hollered, working off their pent-up discontent.

Alvin Karpis acted as a lookout for ferries. The lookout job was pretty small potatoes for a criminal of his caliber, but he relished it, peering out into the black void that was the Bay. A blob of light would appear, inching its way over the Bay. When the small blob materialized into a brilliantly illuminated ferry, Karpis shouted,

"There she blows – let's give 'em a concert!"

Guffaws, whistling and shrieking followed. The din awakened prisoners who hadn't intended to participate in the fracas. They tossed and writhed in their bunks. Unable to sleep, they chimed in. Eventually all 300 prisoners were in the chorus. They screamed their demands.

"We want more privileges – we ain't gonna stop hollering until they hear us in Washington – this ain't a prison – it's a cemetery – we're buried alive."

"We want radios," one prisoner bellowed.

"Yeahhhhhhhh!" they roared in response.

"We want GOOD tobacco."

"Yeahhhhhhhh!"

"We want one movie a week!"

"Yeahhhhhhhh!"

For almost two weeks, they kept up the clamor. Tiring of cursing and roaring, they lapsed into song. It became a raucous, foul-mouthed community sing.

Their favorite songs were sung to the tunes of *Hail, Hail The Gang's All Here* and *Glory, Glory Hallelujah*. First they jeered the warden.

We'll hang old Johnston to a sour apple tree as we go marching on
Glory, glory hallelujah . . .

Right down the line they went, substituting the names of other prison officials.

At the conclusion of each song, the prisoners carried on like a football rooting section – whistling, applauding, and whooping it up – pleased with their performances. Occasionally, various sections of the cellblock divided off and sang individual numbers. The others listened attentively, cheered vigorously.

Guard whistles and the ringing of the regular routine bells provoked the prisoners to their highest pitched screaming. Outbursts often lasted ten unbroken minutes. When throats grew raw from the lung-bursting effort, they saved their voices by resorting to incessant hand clapping. Bound by prison rules to almost endless hours of silence, the prisoners enjoyed the unwonted exercise of their lungs, the noise, and the excitement. It deviated from the deadly routine, even though it meant weeks or months in a disciplinary cell.

Each new striker was ordered to appear before the deputy warden, who held "court" on each individual case.

"So you don't intend to work?" he asked one prisoner who refused to go to his regular job in the mat shop.

"No."

"Why not?"

"We're getting a raw deal here. We're human, just like anybody else. But we're treated like animals – work, eat, sleep – work, eat, sleep."

Another prisoner admitted under questioning that he actually didn't want to strike.

"But," he admitted, "I have to play ball with the other prisoners. You don't live with them. I do."

"What do you expect to get out of this?" the deputy warden demanded.

"Probably nothing. I'm being punished now. If we lose, I will be punished some more. If we win, I will be doing myself a favor."

"You ought to know you can't win out over us."

"I guess you're right. But I can take it. I'm ready to take all you can give me, and more on top of it yet."

The deputy shrugged his shoulders.

"It won't be so funny when all your privileges are gone."

The prisoner sneered.

"Nuts. I'm doing my time straight. I lost all my good behavior credits. I don't give a damn who the hell you are – don't tell me how to do my time."

The deputy motioned to a guard.

"Take him out of here. Throw him in the hole. If he opens his mouth, take him to the dungeon."

Another prisoner was asked why he had not joined in the strike.

"Not me," he explained. "I ain't losing my five years good time."

Good time meant the number of days deducted from a prisoner's sentence because of good behavior.

"I have my own time to do and can't be fooling around with anything else," he continued. "The five years I got will seem like another lifetime."

The warden "got his" on the fourth day of the strike.

This mild-mannered man with the twinkling blue eyes – thoroughly versed in criminal behavior

from his years as warden of Folsom and San
Quentin Penitentiaries – spurned the safety of the
warden's office during the turbulent days of the
strike. He trudged about the Island sizing up the
situation – well aware that supposedly trustworthy
prisoners could seize him as a hostage. He took that
risk.

Visualize what might have happened had a
group of prisoners pounced on him. Using him as a
shield, they might have forced their way through the
gates and attempted to commandeer a launch at the
landing dock. But all of them, even the warden,
would have been mowed down by the tower guard's
machine gun fire before they walked three feet.

The cold, hard laws of Alcatraz held that escape
must be thwarted at any cost. If any civilian
employee, including guard, physician or warden,
became a hostage of escaping prisoners, the civilian
employee must be fired upon to halt the prisoner's
escape.

On the fourth day of the strike, the warden
walked into the mess hall and took up his regular
position alongside the steam table during the noon
meal. This was part of his daily routine, and he
adhered to it even during the hectic days of the
strike. A hundred or so prisoners who had refused to
strike were allowed into the mess hall to eat their
regular meals.

The warden stood by the steam table, arms
folded. His presence was primarily to inspect the
food and let the prisoners know their warden was
interested in them and their welfare. A deputy
warden stood beside him. Row after row of mess

hall benches stood empty. Prisoners who ordinarily occupied them were in the disciplinary cells, being starved into submission. Six slices of bread daily and a regular meal every three days was all the rebels were allowed.

At 11:56 a.m. the deputy warden blew his whistle. The prisoners arose, pushed back their benches, faced the center of the mess hall, and began tramping out in single file. The deputy warden walked toward the mess hall door, the warden lagged behind. Suddenly a prisoner darted out from the end of the line and threw himself on the warden, attacking him from the rear. The prisoner's arms flailed like a windmill as he bludgeoned the warden with his fists. The warden was literally beaten unconscious before he could even turn around and protect himself.

The prisoner – Burton Phillips, a bank robber – sent the warden thudding to the floor with a vicious uppercut then started kicking his prostrate form. In the manner of a football player getting off a long punt, Phillips dug his heavy shoe against the warden's head, his chest, and his back, punctuating each kick with "take that – and that – and that."

Another prisoner attempted to thwart Phillips, but Phillips turned, drove a fist into his face and sent him sprawling. Prisoners still in the mess hall blinked in speechless amazement.

A guard on duty at the far end of the hall sprinted to the scene. Bowling aside the thunderstruck prisoners, he hurled himself on Phillips. They fell to the floor, grappling, gouging and writhing over and over. A second guard arrived and smashed his gas billy against Phillips' head.

Phillips rolled over unconscious, blood spurting from a hole in his scalp. The spectacle of the two guards fighting with Phillips galvanized the stunned prisoners into action. Fearful that the guards might pour a hail of bullets into their midst or that tear gas would cascade down from overhead tanks, they dove under the nearest tables screaming, "Don't shoot – for God's sake, don't shoot."

Suddenly there was the crash-tinkle of breaking glass. It sent them cowering lower under the tables. An outside guard, hearing the commotion, jabbed his sawed off shotgun through the bashed-in window and drew a bead on the unconscious Phillips. Had it not been for other guards who were milling around and the warden who was lying in the line of fire, Phillips might have been riddled with shotgun slugs.

Still unconscious, the warden was lifted from the mess hall floor and carried to the white-walled hospital. His crumpled body was placed on an examining table. I removed the blood from his face and ear with a sterile towel. A swift examination revealed a bleeding nose and a ragged, bleeding laceration of the right ear.

His eyes quivered. Blinking them, he stared at the guards and white-robed members of the hospital staff who hovered over him. Then he asked in a weak voice,

"What did they hit me with, doctor?"

"Just a blow, warden. Do you feel all right?"

"Yes. Who did it?"

"Phillips."

"I didn't see anything. Did he strike me from behind?"

"Yes."

"Am I badly hurt?"

"You'll be all right, warden. It's just a nosebleed and a cut on the ear. Just lie quiet and rest."

The chief medical officer soon arrived and sutured the lacerated ear. He ordered a skull x-ray. No fractures. While this was going on, two guards arrived in an adjoining room bearing the assailant. They tossed him on the floor as though he were a sack of potatoes. He hit with a thump and lay face down. Blood trickled from his torn scalp. He was unconscious for six hours. As he was wheeled into the sterilizing room, a prison official stalked over to his limp form.

The official's face twitched with rage.

"Hit the warden, will you," he ranted. "You . . ."

He grabbed Phillips by the hair, jerked his head up and struck him viciously across the mouth, cutting his lip in several places. Phillips' only reply was a moan. Infuriated, the prison official yanked out his gas billy and swished it through the air, shouting,

"I'll kill you, you dirty rat."

Guards grappled with him, forcing him to drop the gas billy. Wheedling and cajoling him, the official calmed down. Eventually he stomped out of the hospital.

Phillips' scalp was shaved, revealing a three-inch laceration down to the bone. The wound was sutured and dressed. A x-ray revealed no skull fracture. He regained consciousness for a brief second and raised his knee slightly. A guard struck him with a resounding blow across the thigh, hissing,

"Lie still."

When Phillips regained consciousness, he mumbled, "Why don't you do something – shoot me – beat me – kill me – WHY DON'T YOU?"

He was placed in a separate ward and tied down in restraining bedclothes, similar to a straight jacket. The warden was carried by stretcher to his home. Fatigued and stunned though he was, he propped himself up in bed and called Washington and then the press.

Convalescing in the hospital, Phillips later told what prompted the attack.

"I didn't mean to hurt anybody. I didn't hit the warden with anything – just my fists. I did it because they took all my legal papers away from me."

By legal papers he meant the writs on his appeal. Many Alcatraz prisoners whiled away long, dreary hours preparing such writs, acting as their own lawyer. They were not very successful. But working on their own legal papers occupied their minds and they forgot the drab reality about them, confident they would soon win their freedom.

Phillips was doing life for bank robbery and kidnapping. He and a companion robbed the Chandler National Bank at Lyons, Kansas for about $2,000 in 1934. Brandishing guns, they forced two bank employees into a waiting car – presumably so they would not sound the alarm – and then sped away.

The two bank employees were later released some distance from town. Phillips was soon captured. Born in 1912, he was recommended for transfer to Alcatraz "even in the face of his youth, maximum supervision is required." After his recovery and discharge from the hospital, he was sentenced to 19 days in the hole – then placed in isolation.

The strike dragged on. More and more prisoners joined the rebellion and were then brought to the disciplinary cells. Alcatraz officials were in an uncomfortable situation. First, they had to break up the strike and get the prison back to its normal routine. So they cut off food and steam heat and made it otherwise miserable for the locked up strikers. Second, they couldn't risk impairing the prisoner's health. So, the spectacle of an Alcatraz doctor paying daily visits to the unshaven, starved insurrectionists was somewhat ironic.

Twice daily, I made my rounds, visiting each individual cell. The cellblock resembled a beleaguered garrison. The prisoner's faces were matted with beard growth, their eyes bloodshot and sunken. They were gaunt and listless from exhaustion – nights of yammering – and the lack of proper food. They complained of the cold. The air was damp and chilly, for at night the fog swirled around the Rock, and the wind whipped in from the sea. No soothing hiss came from the wall radiators. They hadn't been used for days.

A few prisoners, who assaulted guards, lay naked in their individual cells, hugging themselves for warmth. Many others, whose blankets had been taken away, huddled close to their mattresses, seeking warmth. They wore only drawers, regulation prison coveralls and sox. Shoes were removed because they made deadly weapons.

"Geez doc," they pleaded, "we're freezing – can't you do anything for us – get us blankets or decent grub or heat?"

The cold was beginning to chill their fiery hate, their stubborn resistance. Fog-damp air settled in their cells because windows were ordered open. It numbed their bodies, penetrating their bones. Were these the swaggering bank robbers, brutal kidnappers and two-fisted hoodlums who strutted their bravado in court and in the headlines? Now they whined, "It's cold."

Opening the windows and turning off the heat was one way of bringing the strike to a speedy end. Instead of "turning on the heat," it was literally turned off. Still, the cold presented a health problem. Many were lying in empty cells on icy cement floors. A wholesale epidemic of colds and pneumonia threatened. And, they were human beings.

Soon the radiators were clanking, sputtering and hissing again; warm air circulated through the cells. I asked the warden for more blankets, to have a sufficient number of windows closed, and to maintain an adequate temperature. I stated it wasn't proper to subject the men to any unnecessary exposure.

The hygienic conditions in the cells were deplorable. All water was turned off. It was feared the prisoners might attempt to flood the cells. So for days the lavatories in the cells were not flushed. The prisoners protested. Nothing was done. This, too, was a means of breaking the strike. Drinking water was carried to them in a pail.

On my visits, my pockets were crammed with aspirin, cough drops and sleeping pills. A guard accompanied me from cell to cell. One prisoner ignored the guard's order to "Stir. The doc's here." The prisoner lay in a corner, swathed in a thin blanket, refusing to budge. The guard grunted. Clutching a piece of iron pipe, he said, "Doc – ah – would you step around the corner a second." I obliged. Bodily injury was forbidden on Alcatraz. It could not be inflicted by guards unless in self-defense or to break up a brawl. I knew that if any bodily injury was to be done, I was not supposed to see it. The prisoner was prodded to his feet. I heard some faint thumps. When I turned, the prisoner was up, glaring at the guard.

The rounds continued, always bringing the usual complaints. Some worried about their ringworm, prevalent on the Rock. Others thought they needed their indigestion powder. But I informed them they couldn't have indigestion without meals. One prisoner complained of leg pain. Poor circulation was responsible. I gave him tablets, usually prescribed after meals.

"That's a howl, doc," he chuckled. "I ain't getting any meals."

Most prisoners requested cotton, aspirin and cough drops. The prisoners said their throats grew raw from the nightly yammering and the cough drops were soothing. I suspected they munched on them because of the small bit of food value they contained. Cotton was formed into earplugs to drown out the nightly noise.

I had sound effects to greet my rounds. My appearance on "Broadway" provoked a series of coughs and throat clearings. These throat calisthenics were part of the grapevine code, meaning someone was coming. A blatant "quack-quack-quack" was heard. Others took it up. Soon the cellblock sounded like a busy barnyard. "Machine Gun" Kelly confided that they didn't mean any harm.

"See, doc," he said, "they don't mean to hurt you. It's like this – they razz anybody that passes by and wears a uniform."

On the eighth day, the strike began to weaken. A group of strikers, haggard from the sleepless nights, ravenously hungry, and weak from venting their stored-up wrath, announced they were licked. By the tenth day, the warden was recovered from his injuries and was again at the mess hall.

"I realize the danger of it," he said, "but it's part of my job, and a certain amount of danger goes with the job. It would be poor policy for me to refrain from coming to the mess hall after what happened. The effect upon myself and the prison personnel would be disastrous."

More strikers surrendered each day. The strike officially terminated at the end of two weeks but the leaders were in isolation for a long time. Prison officials emphasized the strikers had gained nothing. But they had. They indulged in a hell-roaring holiday, a break from the deadly routine. It wasn't as successful as the previous strike, prisoners said. For, in that strike, the entire kitchen staff rebelled and guards were forced to cook their own meals.

"Machine Gun" doped it out correctly. I asked, "I thought you said at the end of the last strike that there wouldn't be any more."

He massaged his jaw reflectively and said,

"I guess it's just like a woman having a baby. She promises not to have any more, but a year later she gets another one, anyhow."

ALCATRAZ CAVALCADE

One historic day in August 1775, the Indians who inhabited the shores of San Francisco Bay dropped their stone implements and gaped at a great, white-winged bird floating in through the Golden Gate. The "bird" was the sailing vessel San Carlos, commanded by the Spanish explorer Ayala, the first person to navigate the Bay. Gazing in wonder as they sailed around the world's largest land-locked harbor, the bearded Spaniards noted a small rocky island some three miles inside the heads. From crest to shore, the little rock was covered with raucous, big-billed pelicans, some wheeling overhead, some strutting among the crags, and some nesting.

"Por Dios," exclaimed the doughty Ayala, "those birds are thicker on that island than candles at the foot of an image of Santa Maria! Amigos, we will call this the Isla de los Alcatraces." Alcatraz Island – Island of the Pelicans – is its name to this day.

The pelicans continued to reign there undisturbed until 1846 when Pio Pico, last of the Mexican governors of California, deeded the island to a Yankee settler, Julian Workman.

Workman built a dwelling on the island, plying back and forth between the mainland in a rowboat. Later, desiring to make his son-in-law Mr. Temple a handsome present, Workman deeded the island to him. Temple found little use for the island and, in March 1849, John C. Fremont, soldier of fortune and political explorer, offered him $5,000 for the Rock. Temple accepted.

Fremont signed himself "legal representative of the United States" in making the deal. He later tried to sell it to private interests at a profit but the courts upheld the government's claim to the Island and to the government Alcatraz Island has belonged ever since.

In 1853, Congress decided San Francisco's harbor defenses needed strengthening. Until that time the booming little city's one protection was outmoded Fort Joaquin, built by the Spaniards adjacent to the Presidio. A congressional bill provided for two new forts to be built on opposite shores of the Golden Gate, and two more forts on the larger islands of the Bay, Angel and Alcatraz Islands.

Alcatraz was to be the last word in modern fortresses. The Army sent its engineers to the Island in July 1853. "Here," they said, "we will blast the sloping sides away to make them perpendicular and more impregnable to an enemy landing party. There, we will build trenches and protect them with cannons from above. Over there, on the northeast shore, we will place the landing wharf because there the island is most accessible. [The landing wharf has remained there to this day.] To protect the road to the landing wharf, we will build a shot-proof guardhouse with a drawbridge."

Further engineering plans called for a formidable brick-and-granite fortress to rise on the brow of the Island and the installation of 91 guns. These were to be delivered into three batteries. The first would draw a bead on any enemy man o'war entering the Golden Gate; the second and third would rain fire on the ship channels on either side of the Island.

People from San Francisco's Chinatown, destitute gold panners from the gold fields, trappers and adventurers, were hired by the Army to build the fortification. Some of the granite was brought from China. By 1859, the defense was officially completed and Fort Alcatraz looked proudly over San Francisco Bay.

The Army worried about a lengthy siege – where would they store the food, water, gunpowder, and cannon balls? The solution was a honeycomb of underground brick-and-stone cells and corridors. The Army masons built well and those same cells still stand – little altered save for new coats of plaster and cement. They became the dungeons of Alcatraz.

As far back as 1854, Alcatraz had a lighthouse. The lantern sat on an octagonal base towering 214 feet above the waves and was visible for 21 miles at sea. It was the first lighthouse to be placed in commission on the Bay. It remained one of the most important. A straight line could be drawn from Alcatraz to the lightship just outside the Golden Gate and then to the lighthouse on the Farallon Islands – 30 miles away. A ship that placed itself on this line rode snugly into San Francisco harbor, directly in the middle of the ship channel.

By 1907, modern marine warfare and big guns rendered the haughty fortress obsolete. Congress ruled that Alcatraz was to become a military prison or "disciplinary barracks." A new prison building went up with a cellblock large enough for 600 prisoners. That cellblock, completed in 1909, was the same cellblock – with some additional safeguards – that housed America's most notable public enemies.

As this new era for Alcatraz began, solider-prisoners in drab denim supplanted the trim blue uniforms that had swarmed the Island. Heavy as the punishing hand of the Army lay on its transgressors, it was not so heavy as the hand of Uncle Sam on later-day gangsters and criminals.

Many Army prisoners achieved the status of trustees. They had the run of the Island and went about their tasks in plain view of curious ferryboat commuters. Gangs of prisoners worked on the mainland, in the Presidio, or on the Army transport docks.

Nor was escape as difficult in Army days. Prisoners made successful getaways seven times during the Army's occupation. The first one occurred when three Civil War prisoners dashed down to the water's edge, jumped into a rowboat and escaped. That was before the new Army prison went up.

A "weeping widow" made another spectacular escape. One day, an Army officer died. His sorrowing widow ordered a mourning costume from San Francisco. Weeping under her heavy black veil, the widow tottered decorously onto the shore boat. The sentry did not have the heart to ask the lady for her pass. The sentry on the mainland felt the same way. It was not until several hours later when the real widow wanted to know why her mourning ensemble had not arrived that the abashed authorities learned the weeping lady was an escaped prisoner.

Another time three daring trustees skipped with forged pardons. They were doing clerical work in the prison office. Waiting until the commanding officer was absent on shore leave, they forged his signature on three pardons and slipped them into the incoming mail. The "pardons" caused surprise among the office staff. Because the documents appeared genuine enough, nobody questioned them. Amid congratulations and well wishes, the trio boldly boarded the shore boat. To allay any suspicions by the dock sentry on land, they forged three shore passes. The dock sentry became suspicious and started to make a report. The three ran. One escaped but the other two became loquacious in a San Francisco saloon and were apprehended.

During the Indian wars, many an obstreperous Indian chieftain found his way into the military prison. One of them was an Apache Chief, Kaete-na, friend of the infamous Geronimo. His own tribesmen tried Kaete-na for instigating trouble on the Indian reservation. They sentenced him to a three-year term at Alcatraz.

Records show that the Army diplomatically tried to get rid of Alcatraz for 30 years. As far back as 1906, General Frederick Funston reported to the government that he thought Alcatraz was unsuited and inadequate for prison purposes. He recommended that the prison be transferred to

Angel Island. In 1933, the War Department finally declared it no longer had any use for Alcatraz Island. Then, the Department of Justice bespoke for Alcatraz. It had been thinking for some time about a prison where the most incorrigible offenders could be segregated.

Attorney General Homer Cummings first outlined the new scheme publicly on October 12, 1933. He declared that Alcatraz was to house the type of prisoners who were confirmed jail breakers, troublemakers, the "dangerous, vicious and irredeemable." These, said Mr. Cummings, comprised between three and four percent of the 18,000 prisoners.

Plans immediately converted Alcatraz into what the Department of Justice classified as a prison of "super-maximum security for incorrigible and long-term offenders." [Atlanta and Leavenworth rated only as "maximum security," McNeil Island as "medium security" and work camps as "minimum security."]

The old 600 soft steel cell fronts were ripped out and replaced by tool-proof steel with automatic-locking devices. Tear gas outlets, new guard towers connected by overhead walks, floodlights, barbed wire fences, electric snitches (metal detectors) and a host of other devices were installed. The guards were picked from other prisons. They were schooled for three months on McNeil Island. There they learned how to box, wrestle, detect coded messages, find smuggled objects, quell riots, short-circuit a prison grapevine and detect the underworld telegraph system.

An intricate telephone system was installed. Every spot on the Island, from the dock to the guard towers, was linked to the exchange in Warden Johnston's office. A separate trunk line connected Alcatraz with the mainland. But the authorities did not depend on telephone alone. A short-wave radio station was set-up in a bulletproof building. It was to be used in case the main trunk was cut. At specified times, signals were exchanged between the guard on duty at the short wave station and the Coast Guard. Coast Guard officials stood ready to dispatch a boat the moment one of these signals failed to come through. In a pinch, Alcatraz authorities could call on local police boats as well as airplanes.

To prevent a repetition of the escape at nearby San Quentin in 1925 [when 19 trustees escaped in a commercial tugboat tied up at the prison dock] only Army tugs were allowed to land on the Island. No other vessel was allowed within 200 yards – and drifting objects were shot.

That Alcatraz was probably America's cleanest penitentiary might be due to the high standard of sanitation and cleanliness set by the Army. Water was brought over in barges, as the Island had no water supply of its own. Many of the prison workshops were the same ones operated by Army prisoners.

When Alcatraz stood ready to receive its new prisoners in August 1934, the horrible memory of the Kansas City massacre was still fresh. When agents were transferring Frank Nash – who escaped from Leavenworth 18 months before – from

Arkansas back to Leavenworth, the 7:30 a.m. train into the Kansas City station was met by gangsters that swooped down on them, spraying bullets. Four agents were murdered, two were wounded, and Nash was killed. Although there were crowds at the station, the gangsters escaped.

To avoid similar occurrences, the government made plans for the first Alcatraz transfer as carefully and secretly as a field general on the eve of a decisive campaign. Prisoners were picked from Atlanta, Leavenworth and McNeil Island. The starting point was Atlanta. A departure day was set and then intentionally changed.

On the appointed day, prisoners were roused in their cells and spirited away. Under heavy guard, they were marched aboard two Pullman railroad cars with steel-barred windows. Shades were permanently drawn as the train streaked over specially cleared tracks with its cargo of human freight. None knew their ultimate destination.

Another Pullman accommodated the Army relief guards who flanked the train every time it stopped.

By a secret route unknown even to railroad officials, the train arrived at the small hamlet of Benicia, several miles north of San Francisco Bay. Here the railroad-prison was re-routed over a rusty obsolete local line to Tiburon, a tiny village on the Bay.

On what was to be their last day on the train, the prisoners noticed complete silence, yet their coach was moving with a swaying, rocking motion.

They peeked through the shades and saw they were on a barge. All about them was gray water. In the distance they saw a squat island with massed stone buildings and knew they were destined for Alcatraz – the government's highly touted Devil's Island. Those stone buildings looked as stark as headstones, marking a living tomb for many.

The news had leaked out to the Bay newspapers. Reporters on launches tried to crowd close to the floating prison. But they were shooed away by Coast Guard cutters and warned not to approach within 300 feet.

When the train barge reached the Alcatraz wharf, the prisoners were marched in small groups through the electric snitch, and then whisked up to their new home in a prison wagon.

The transfer was made without a single mishap. In Washington, jittery officials sighed with relief when they heard by telegram that the "bamboo cosmos" – the code name for the prison train – arrived safely and all the "furniture" deposited without a scratch. When Warden Johnston thought that the train might not arrive until after mealtime, he wired Washington and asked that the "furniture" be well "oiled" before being discharged. By oiled, he meant fed.

Original cannon atop "Fort Alcatraz."

Shaped like a battleship, its nose pointing northwest toward the Marin Hills, Alcatraz Island juts out of San Francisco Bay three miles inside the Golden Gate and one and one-half miles from the nearest landing point in San Francisco.

It was the crest of a submarine mountain. From a distance, the Rock looked like a small, tawny crag surmounted by the steel-barred prison and the towering white lighthouse. Closer inspection revealed numerous houses, roads, trees, shrubbery and vivid patches of flowers. About 130 feet high, the Rock was 12 acres in extent, 525 feet wide and 1750 feet long.

Visitors began their trip to Alcatraz Island from the Fort Mason pier in San Francisco. There they boarded the government launch. Most were impressed with the forbidding loneliness and brooding air of secrecy. This was somewhat dispelled by the sight of green foliage and smoke curling from the chimneys of little houses. Huge forbidding letters were painted upon the cliffs, on the roofs and sides of buildings: ALCATRAZ – WARNING, KEEP OFF! This reminded visitors that one was approaching America's sternest penitentiary.

At the water's edge were rows of barbed wire fences. Enclosed towers, mounted high on slender steel legs, provided a perch for the guards and their automatic rifles.

The launch crept into the buoy-marked zone past which all other crafts were forbidden to approach. If a vessel tried to approach, it was greeted with a volley of shots from the guard towers.

The little dock bustled with activity as the government launch prepared to snuggle into its berth. Men in gray coveralls and gray caps, with numbers over their hearts and on their backs – excellent rifle targets – tugged at freight on roller carts. Watching over them was a man in blue. When the steam whistle shrilled, men in gray dropped their work. A lieutenant in the dock office barked a command and the men scurried to one side until the boat departed. No prisoner ever got within 50 feet of that escape route.

Popping out of nowhere, guards swarmed over the dock as the visitors walked down the gangplank. Each one was scrutinized with a cold, hard stare.

"Got a pass? Who are you coming to see?" asked the guard at the foot of the gangplank. Anyone who did not pass muster got no further than the dock. There the visitor was held in custody until the launch departed.

The visitor was led through an electric metal detector, or the "hot dog stand." This device established an oscillatory circuit or field, comparable to the waves from a radio transmitter. It was tuned to a certain electrostatic capacity that was violently disturbed by any metal on the person who passed into the circuit. Even a minute piece of metal concealed in a person's ear could be detected. An uncoiled watch spring was good material for a saw.

Anyone who made the hot dog stand "bark" was searched until the metal was found.

After the visitor passed the test, an official telephoned from the dock to the prison office to verify that the visitor was expected. Then, under surveillance, the visitor was escorted to the prison in a black patrol wagon. The paved roads dated from Army days. In the steepest parts, cross-grooves were cut into the cement. During the Army's occupation of the Island, mules were the principal means of transportation; their hoofs were able to obtain a firm foothold in the grooves.

With the motor roaring in low gear, the wagon passed under an old Spanish archway, then around a sharp bend. It sometimes threw visitors from their seats. Another steep climb. Another sharp turn. The visitor glimpsed moss and trickling water seeping through a natural rock wall. On the terraced hillsides were broad carpets of sturdy green ice plant, covered in the spring with brilliant magenta flowers. Cypress and eucalyptus trees were abundant.

On the next turn, the visitor eyed the glistening steel bars covering every window and opening of the prison. Prisoners working on the outside detail stood aside to let the car continue its climb.

Now they were at the top. The rear doors of the wagon opened and the visitor stood before the doors of the prison. Over the entrance hung a great emblem of the American flag and Uncle Sam's eagle. Large letters spelled "Administration Building."

The visitor was escorted up the steps and through the door, where he encountered the electric snitch. Officials passed a few words with the visitor. Then the visitor was given a thorough shakedown. Clothes, wallet, and packages were examined. If the visitor was "clean," an official signaled a guard in the Armory.

Through a small, glass-covered opening and with the aid of a large mirror set up at a 135-degree angle, the guard in the Armory could see everyone entering and leaving the main and cellhouse gates. Only by his authorization could anyone pass through the main gate of the Armory's tool-proof steel.

A small buzzer notified the guard that somebody wanted to pass through the gate. A glance in the mirror showed him who it was. He pulled a small catch lever. It caused two large metal plates to slide on the main gate, exposing a large keyhole. A large key was inserted from the other side of the gate. The barrier swung open and was shut again by means of lever and key.

The visitor and his escort were locked in a huge metal cage, ten feet wide and 20 feet long. They were surrounded by steel and a bare, highly polished floor. At one end were thick, bulletproof windows, a mere six inches wide and 18 inches long. Through one of these small apertures the visitor caught a glimpse of the imprisoned friend or relative.

Thirty minutes, once a month, was the stringent rule for all visitors. No embrace or personal contact was possible through the glass and steel. The guards accompanying both visitor and prisoner overheard everything that was said. Small chance for either prisoner or visitor to say anything off the record, unless they worked out a secret code using innocent-sounding words. Metal partitions ensured some visual privacy. Oral privacy was not possible because loud talking was necessary to be heard through the steel perforations. Human emotions surmounted the steel and glass, revealing themselves in voice, gesture and eye, in the clutched handkerchief and the drooping shoulder.

Often good-byes were hard to say but the guards were strict. The visitor watched the prisoner shuffle down the long, steel-barred corridor until he was out of sight. Then the visitor was hustled off.

Outside, the wagon waited. Down the steep hills, around the sharp curves, past cliffs and rocks. Once more through the Spanish archway and then to the dock, where the visitor signed out under the cold surveillance of the guards.

The visitors' launch always left San Francisco at 10 a.m. At 11:20 a.m., the visitor was back on board, the whistle shrieked, the launch trembled, nosed out and the visit to Alcatraz was over.

Visitors approach the Administration Building led by a guard. My father identified the visitors as "Mrs. Capone and brother Ralph."

LIVING ON THE ROCK

Life on the Rock was not confined to the stone prison walls. There were pretty, cozy houses where the prison staff lived and an apartment house occupied by more than 50 families. The warden, medical officers, and sub-chiefs of the custodial force occupied the dwellings near the crest of the Island. These buildings were once designated for the Army's commanding officers. My wife and I occupied one of these houses.

The apartment house was the erstwhile soldier's barracks. It was partitioned into suitable apartments for secretaries and clerks, their wives and children, and separate bachelor quarters. There was a long wait for vacant houses and apartments.

Residents were permitted to have visitors freely but accompanied the visitor to and from the dock.

There were many children on the Island whose laughter echoed along the grim walls. They played along the roads as if Alcatraz were some quiet suburb. School meant daily excursions across the Bay to San Francisco. The 7:40 a.m. boat was the school boat. The 3:15 and 4:00 p.m. boats conveyed the children back to the Island.

The former Army parade ground was the children's favorite playground. There they ran, jumped, played ball and roller-skated. Like all youngsters, they liked to play cops and robbers. But toy weapons were not permitted. Authorities figured a prisoner with a toy weapon could stage a successful break for freedom. So they destroyed the play weapons.

Whizzing down the steep inclines of the Rock on roller coasters was another juvenile sport. Sometimes, when they managed to elude parental vigilance, the youngsters rambled along the cliffs, climbing where footholds would hardly accommodate a goat.

During their play, children often came into close contact with the prisoners working on the outdoor details. The children were warned that the men in gray denim were "bad men" and were told not to go near them. An inquisitive child occasionally approached while they were working.

"What are you making, mister?"

"Building a wall, sonny," was the polite reply.

One day someone observed a prisoner in the outside detail taking care of the flowerbeds. The prisoner came upon a rabbit in one of the gardens. The rabbit was very tame.

The prisoner called the rabbit to him. Making sure he wasn't being observed, the prisoner knelt down and stroked the animal. This was a rare pleasure for a prisoner. Looking around like a mischievous child about to be caught with his hand in the cookie jar, he picked up the animal and petted it to the enjoyment of both. When he heard approaching footsteps, he quickly dropped the rabbit and continued with his work.

Of course, the inevitable guard on every work detail was there to protect the children from any possible harm. But the guard was unnecessary. Prisoners were notoriously "soft" where children were concerned. They loved to see them playing about – it made them forget the stern reality of prison. They would play with the children if they could. Having a child talk to him was a special event in any prisoner's life.

The children went to weekly Sunday school that was organized and maintained by the women on the Island. On alternate Sunday evenings, the prison chaplain held non-denominational services for residents of the Island in the canteen building. This building housed the general store and post office, and was a meeting place in the evening. Residents enjoyed parties, bingo, children's Christmas plays, and dances in its main hall. Orchestras were hired from San Francisco for the dances.

Adjoining the main hall was the chess-checker-and-card room. In the floor below were bowling alleys, pool tables and a gym.

Men held bowling tournaments and divided into teams. High rivalry developed and for weeks bowling was the main topic. On tournament nights, the spectator's gallery filled to capacity. Often the women bowled.

The Officer's Club maintained recreational activities. It held regular meetings in the canteen. Dues and proceeds were used to install and maintain the equipment as well as provide refreshments for the various functions. Everyone attended these functions, though no alcohol, not even beer, was permitted. Prisoners cleaned up after functions.

Usually it was too windy to play tennis, but many men liked to play handball on the parade ground. The prisoners built a new, enclosed handball court and here the more active guards kept their waistlines down. Fishing at various points was a favorite sport, particularly when the bass were running.

At night the movements of the Island residents were more restricted. Guards patrolled all night, playing powerful lights on any movement in the dark and flashing their signals to one another. Just after sundown, a guard toured the Island to turn on all outside lights. Dead lamps were replaced immediately.

Cars driven at night exchanged signals with the tower guards. Drivers signaled by flashing headlights on and off a specified number of times. This assured the tower guard that the vehicle was driven by a guard and not by an escaping prisoner.

As boats arrived or departed at night, the dock was flooded with noonday brilliance by the dock tower light. A guard patrolled the small pier. All arriving and departing boats were examined from cabin to hold to make sure there were no stowaways.

Every individual living on the Island had a pass. When leaving, the pass was placed in the "out" file in the dock office; when returning, the pass was dropped in the "in" file. Passes were counted and records kept of everyone coming on and off the Island.

Guards and their families lived in this apartment house.

Children played on the swing and slide (lower right) in the shadow of the prison.

COME AND GET IT

Long gray lines of prisoner backs hunched over the polished tables of the Alcatraz mess hall. Nervously and rapidly, the eaters slung down food from the metal dishes – like men with only a few minutes to catch a train. Twenty minutes was allotted for a meal and any man who wasn't finished when the whistle sounded went hungry.

The air was stifling. Odors from the steam tables mingled with the odors of perspiring human bodies. Every window was shut to allow for the greater efficacy of tear gas bombs.

It was noisy with the clatter of tin ware, utensils, and the sound of munching. But no word was spoken outside of a grunted "wouldja pass me the salt," or "give us another hunk of bread." All other talking was forbidden.

Hawk-like vigilance was maintained over every movement in the mess hall, from passing pepper to lifting a spoon. Eight guards wove in and out among the tables – watching.

At the east end of the gun gallery – where the electric controls of the tear gas bombs were also located – stood an armed guard – watching. On the catwalk outside the north wall of the hall, a guard paced with rifle in hand – watching. Outside the main entrance of the hall stood six guards – watching. In a chair sat a deputy warden – watching.

Alcatraz boasted the best meals of any prison. The food was hygienically prepared, the menus were nicely varied, and a prisoner could order all he wanted. Yet a larger percentage of prisoners suffered from indigestion, nervous stomachs, and other gastric disturbances than in any other prison. Why? Perhaps it was the nervous tension of being watched by the guards and the short period allotted for meals.

Any day's menu included hot breads, fresh vegetables, delicatessen dishes, crisp salads, ice cream, choice roasts, rich soups and fancy desserts. The Rock was harsh and stingy in other ways but where food was concerned, it was lavish. Why? Poor food or an insufficiency of it was one of the prime instigators of a general strike or mess hall riot. And strikes, chief horror of Alcatraz authorities, were common. Most of the prisoners figured they had nothing to lose anyway.

At meal times the cell doors clanged open. Prisoners fell into double lines and marched into the mess hall, passing directly to the steam tables at one end, where the food was served cafeteria style. There they saw all the dishes before them – a steaming cauldron of soup, mounds of vegetables, the meat entrée, and the salad. Bread and dessert were already on the tables.

Each prisoner was handed a metal tray, divided into partitions for the various foods. Soup, coffee, tea and water were served in metal cups and bowls. As he passed along the steam tables, the prisoner asked for what he wanted. Prisoner-servers dished out his food. He might ask for all the dishes, skip some, or order double portions of others. But there was one inflexible rule. A prisoner must eat everything on his tray or get nothing the next meal.

With laden trays, the prisoners marched to the tables, filling up all the places on one side of the mess hall first, then the other. As soon as they sat down, they began to shovel it in. Every minute counted if a prisoner wanted the dessert beckoning him from the center of the table. The fastest gobblers were the prisoners who entered the mess hall at the end of the line. These unlucky ones lost ten minutes eating time while they waited for their comrades to be served. A prisoner's place in line was determined by the location of his cell. Often the frantic wolfing of food by a prisoner at the end of a line and the resulting damage to his digestion caused me to request a change of cell for him. Only the toughest stomachs could tolerate the punishment.

The few who finished eating before the rest sat silently, hands clasped on the table where the guards could see them. When the deputy warden blew the whistle, the diners dropped everything, rose, and noisily pushed back the benches. All utensils – the dull knives, forks and spoons that were laid at every place – were passed to the end of the table and counted before the prisoners left the hall. If even a single spoon was missing, the whistle sounded a warning.

"All right, who's got that spoon," a guard would say. Failure to produce it resulted in an immediate shakedown.

For double precaution, the prisoners passed through the electric mess hall snitch. A spoon or fork could easily be fashioned into a deadly weapon. Leaving the mess hall, the prisoners marched in rows of four, back to the four main rows of cells. The prisoners that marched in last marched out first.

The mess hall was located at the west end of the cellhouse. Tables were of polished wood, mounted on metal legs. Benches were also wood, on an iron pipe frame. Five prisoners could sit on one bench. There was plenty of light and sweeping views of the Bay courtesy of the spacious, albeit steel-barred windows that reached almost to the ceiling. Beyond the steam tables was the large kitchen with its white-tiled floor, great stoves, griddles, ovens, and huge kettles for soups and stews. There were modern, scientific machines for washing dishes and tableware.

Behind the kitchen was a pantry for the chief steward, who was a member of the penitentiary staff, and his assistant, who supervised the officer's mess hall. This was where all the full-time government employees ate. Underneath the kitchen was a storeroom for groceries and meats. Next to this was the shakedown cage where food and other materials were examined in the presence of a guard to prevent smuggling. In this region was also the prison bakery.

The prisoners did the actual cooking and baking, under strict sanitary conditions and constant supervision. Five prisoners worked in the kitchen as cooks for the prisoner's food. Two other prisoners prepared the food for the officer's mess hall. Four prisoners served as bakers. Three worked in the vegetable room – peeling, picking, rinsing, slicing, and chopping. Three prisoners were butchers in the prison ice plant. One prisoner was employed in the storeroom.

Four prisoners worked at the kitchen dish tanks, feeding the dishwashing machines, drying the metal trays, bowls, and cutlery. Four prisoners worked in the mess hall where they set the tables, filled salt, pepper, and sugar shakers before standing behind the steam tables and dishing out the food. After meals were over, these prisoners gathered the soiled utensils, scrubbed the tables and mopped the floor.

Hospital patients were given the same meals as the rest of the prisoners unless the prison doctor ordered a special diet.

A typical menu follows:

Breakfast
   Cereal
   Hot rolls, margarine
   Stewed prunes
   Coffee, milk and sugar
Dinner
   Tomato rice soup
   Individual meat rolls, Creole sauce
   Mashed potatoes and string beans
Supper
   Fresh beef stew with vegetables
   Lettuce salad
   Hot biscuit, margarine
   Ginger cake and tea

Prisoners worked on the catwalk with the deputy warden (right) nearby.

Sick Line

"Next!"

Face after face passed before me. It was sick line time, when any prisoner with any medical complaint came to the hospital for aid. I saw the pale blank faces of prisoners with a serious medical problem; the pouting, frowning faces of prisoners who wanted to be sick but weren't; the faces of whiners who wanted to be coddled. One by one they passed in review, stated their complaint, and passed on.

"There's something the matter with my ear, doc."

"Wait outside and I'll look at it. Next!"

"I'm bothered with that indigestion, doc."

"Don't eat any breakfast tomorrow. I'll have you up for an examination. Next!"

"Say, doc, my scalp itches. I have dandruff and I'm losing all my hair. I think I'm going bald."

"Can't do anything for falling hair."

"But can't I have some mineral oil? I used to rub it on my hair before I got sent here. It helped it fine."

"Mineral oil is for constipation, not for hair. Next!"

"Headache, doc."

"Get some aspirin over there. Next!"

"It's that same trouble in my stomach again, doc. If there's something wrong inside of me, cut it out. I don't care. I've been cut before."

"Wait for an examination. Next!"

"How about taking this wart off for me, doc?"

"I'll take care of it later in the week. Next!"

"Doc, I've got a rash on my body – here, see. I think it's from eating that rice pudding. I never could stand rice."

"Why did you eat it?"

"Well, I had to eat it. Otherwise they wouldn't have given me anything the next meal."

"Wait over there. Next!"

"My face is dry. Can I have something to use after I shave?"

"No. We have no face lotion. Next!"

"I need a physic, doc."

"Over there. Next!"

"Next! Next! Next!"

The parade of the sick and would-be sick went on and on. The sick line was held daily following the noon meal, when the prisoners had a brief rest period. Thus they came to the hospital on their own time. If a prisoner needed a thorough examination, he was excused from work and reported to the hospital.

The sick line was only part of the prison hospital staff's work. Any moment some bleeding or slashed guard or prisoner might be brought in, giving the hospital an emergency room appearance. Such was the case one afternoon when a guard was brought in bleeding profusely from the nose and side of the face.

"I was down in the kitchen basement," he gasped. "Some prisoners jumped me. One of them started letting me have it with a shiv (knife). The others held me as he started cutting me up . . ."

Examination disclosed stab wounds in the left
check, on the bridge of the nose, three on the chest
and two in the abdomen. It was learned that the
prisoner who did the slashing had been reported
previously for homosexual activities by the guard.
The prisoners involved were placed in solitary
confinement. The slasher was later transferred to
isolation and confined there for months.

The quiet associated with a hospital was found
in the Alcatraz hospital. But other times, violence
flared up as patients indulged in knockdown and
drag-out battles. One of the most hectic days started
when one prisoner called another a rat.

"Who's a rat!" the other fumed.

And they were upon each other. One broke
away and sprinted to a window, where he grabbed a
three-foot iron rod used to open the windows. Then,
running back to his opponent, he started raining
blows on him. One vicious smash resulted in a
three-inch deep wound on the forehead and another
pierced the shoulder.

Unable to ward off the blows, the hapless
opponent backed away, took a running jump, leaped
on the prisoner who was wielding the bar, got his
hands around his throat and started throttling him. A
guard rushed in and with some effort separated
them.

Attempts of prisoners feigning sickness were
common – so they could get out of working in the
shops or transfer out of Alcatraz. One prisoner
almost succeeded in getting transferred to a less
strict penitentiary by feigning active tuberculosis. It
was discovered he was giving us the "borrowed"

sputum of a prisoner with an active case of tuberculosis.

Alcatraz was probably the cleanest institution of its kind. The prisoners themselves were subjected to compulsory hygienic conditions. Their clothes were laundered and repaired weekly.

A prisoner's wardrobe was sparse. It consisted of two pieces of underwear – one a heavy shirt with sleeves, the other drawers with full-length legs – several pairs of white socks, large blue handkerchiefs, and two pairs of one-piece button-front coveralls, gray for workdays and blue for holidays.

The kitchen staff wore trousers of the same grayish material with white shirts open at the throat, and aprons. Each prisoner was allotted two pair of shoes. One was worn at work, the other on Sundays and holidays. They took particular pride in keeping their shoes well shined; there was an unlimited supply of shoe polish.

Beneath the cellblocks was a large room with approximately forty stall showers. Once a week, all prisoners – except the kitchen staff – were compelled to take showers unless ordered not to for medical reasons. The prisoners were taken to the showers in groups of five and ten. Many prisoners complained they wanted more showers but the rules held they were entitled to only one per week.

Prisoners employed in the kitchen and officer's mess showered daily. They were examined periodically to see that they were free from disease. All cases of prisoners with tuberculosis were removed from the kitchen and given work elsewhere, preferably on the outside details.

Prisoners brought their dirty clothes to the shower area, deposited the bundles, and brought clean laundry back to their cells.

Haircuts were offered once a month. Hair was clipped short by the prisoner-barbers. Some completely shaved their heads at their own request, because of itching or ringworm of the scalp.

Prisoners shaved themselves three times a week. Safety razor blades were distributed before each shave and collected again when finished. The blades were kept in pieces of cardboard containing the prisoner's number.

A cellhouse orderly distributed each blade. The men shaved within seven minutes and, as no hot water was available in the cells, cold water sufficed. Then the orderly returned and collected each blade.

Prisoners standing on the Alcatraz Island dock.

LITERARY AND SOCIAL CLUB

Alcatraz had its prisoner version of a Literary and Social Club. Only it was all done undercover. The gossip and poetry wasn't confined merely to one afternoon a week – it went on continually. And the gossip and poetry, instead of being distributed over teacups and iced cakes and sandwiches, was usually meted out via the grapevine – or prisoner communications system.

Prisoners established an elaborate grapevine because of the rigorous no-talking rule. Extensive code systems were devised and news or gossip was relayed by gestures, coughing or sneezing, tapping, or through the prison library books.

The library book method was the simplest. It principally conveyed messages to prisoners in isolation. A library book listed each prisoner's number in the front, showing the order in which he could obtain the book. The list was written in pencil. A prisoner in possession of the book carefully went through it and lightly underlined certain words on succeeding pages. He then erased the number following his own and inserted the number of the prisoner for whom the message was intended.

The grapevine was used mostly in the cellblock, where talking was prohibited. Say a choice morsel of news broke one evening. Rather than save it for the next day, when it could be passed around verbally in the shops or in the yard, the prisoners immediately distributed it via the coughing, sneezing, and tapping method.

The literary club aspects were due to the way poetry flourished on Alcatraz. Many prisoners batted off page after page of crude-rhyming stanzas on the slightest provocation. The poems were made in book form and were widely distributed among the prisoners.

Prisoners hailed *One Mile Out in the Bay* as a masterpiece.

One Mile Out in the Bay
by Arthur T. McDonald #109
[who called himself Senator Mack]

The G-men are relentless
That's of Edgar Hoover's Clan
For every crime committed
You can bet they get a man.

So we are out on Devil's Island
In the Heart of Frisco Bay
Where they send public enemies
To pine their life away.

As a prisoner on the Island
I have heard of every crime
So do not interrupt me
While I put each one in rhyme.

Long after I have left this place
My memory shall keep
Firm recollection of the cell
Wherein I used to sleep.

I cannot cast the thought aside
From my retentive brain
But will tread the straight and narrow path
And never go back again.

For my cell is awfully lonely
And the walls are very plain
And on my door you will find a number
That they gave me for my name.

I can't forget the boys I met
Within those dreary walls
Nor of the stories that they told
Of their glories and their falls.

I have heard the tales of kidnappers
With plans carried out by stealth
And dreams of easy money
With a hope to roll in wealth.

The mail robber with his level guns
Who cries, "Throw up your hands"
Now sits alone in sorrow
When in Alcatraz he lands.

The bank robbers who have preyed upon
Those many National Banks
With all their bold and clever schemes
They come to join our ranks.

The murderer, who in vengeful mood
Had fired that fatal shot
God only knows his state of mind
Or what may be his lot.

The confidence man who swindled widows
And the trusting poor
Is given time to meditate
Behind these steel barred doors.

Now the income tax evaders
Well you can't call that a crime
Yet they sent Capone to Alcatraz
To finish up his time.

Now in rhyme you have heard my story
Of all these different crimes
And it deals with men at Alcatraz
Who are serving out their time.

But, strange to say, all we guys
Come down here with a song
"I did not pull that stunt at all
They've got me sized up wrong."

Now Alcatraz from Frisco
Is one mile out in the Bay
But Frisco from Alcatraz is years and years away.

The prison gossip bandied about Alcatraz mostly concerned humorous or interesting happenings. The prisoners relished the story about a fellow prisoner who was having his tonsils removed. He eyed the surgeon and his assistant who were wearing masks and grunted, "You guys look like bank robbers."

Other items that interested them were reports on injuries suffered by guards or prisoners in brawls. Homemade weapons were also discussed.

One of the stories they told at Alcatraz was how a guard lost his whistle after the prison opened. Every cell and prisoner was shaken down but the whistle wasn't found – and was never found. Several times a week, the whistle was heard during the eerie quiet of the cellhouse night. Guards scurried up and down, searching for it, as the prisoners jeered and laughed.

Prisoners on the clean-up crew watered and weeded my father's garden.

SUFFER LITTLE CHILDREN

"You know," said a prisoner, "the first Christmas I was here on the Rock, I didn't even know it was Christmas. We were told to put on our blue holiday clothes and I wanted to know what for. Christmas, I was told. Aw hell, it ain't Christmas, I said – if it was, we would get a sack of candy like when we were back at Leavenworth."

Christmas was observed on Alcatraz as it might be observed by some snow-bound polar expedition – without holly, without radios blaring *Peace on Earth, Good Will Toward Men*, without green and red gift packages.

As the holiday season approached, a change was noticed in the prisoner's behavior and attitude. Many became content and happy. Others moped around with a touch of remorsefulness. They were the ones who thought of home and family, and of previous Christmas days with blazing fires and festive meals.

Some prisoners festooned their cells with gay-colored Christmas-time pictures, torn from the pages of magazines. Most of them were advertisements. They hung pictures on the blank concrete walls – Santa Clauses with bulging packs of a certain brand of cigarette; bowls containing seas of snowy Tom and Jerry's; realistic-looking plum puddings; and quarts of whiskey in holiday wrappings.

Some prisoners hung up their socks on Christmas Eve, knotting them around the cell door bars. I asked one prisoner what he hoped to receive in his sock.

"Oh," he grinned, "maybe a couple of grains of morphine and a shot of whiskey. But I wouldn't bank on it. They wouldn't let Santa Claus in here without a pass, just like any other visitor. And besides, he couldn't wedge his way through all the electric snitches – he's too fat. And once he did get inside, he couldn't crash through all the steel doors they have in this place."

There was a movie on Christmas Day, just as there was on all legal holidays. And there was turkey. Many overate and became ill, asking for soda to settle their stomachs.

The harshness that was Alcatraz seemed to soften somewhat on Christmas. Even the guards became imbued with the holiday spirit. Quite a few guards reported to work on Christmas morning with pockets full of candy. Now candy, of course, was just as impossible to find as narcotics on the Island. It was forbidden among the prisoners. Yet some guards placed the candy in certain locations, and the prisoners would suddenly look up and be surprised to find a few pieces within their reach.

In the hospital, Christmas candy was placed on the table in the main ward. In orderly fashion, each patient walked to the table, took several pieces and returned to their places. Appreciation came not in words but in smiles. What a treat this was on Alcatraz. To feel something sweet in one's mouth – to chew it – to crunch it – to swallow it!

Following the turkey dinner, another surprise awaited the hospital patients. Factory-made cigarettes – one for each patient – were placed on the table.

Like candy, cigarettes were prohibited. Hospital prisoners' eyes bulged with expectancy as they ambled to the table, picked one up, and proceeded to sit down and enjoy a good smoke. Contentment reigned as clouds of blue smoke – so characteristic of these cigarettes – were blown into the air from elevated heads.

The harsh tobacco provided by the government left the prisoners unsatisfied. Their privileges allowed for pipes or cigarettes or both. They were issued as much pipe or cigarette tobacco as they wished. Cigarettes were hand-rolled. Prisoners made a none-too-satisfactory concoction by mixing the pipe and cigarette tobacco together. In desperation, some were known to grind up aspirin tablets into a fine powder and mix it with their tobacco to get a "lift" or a "bang" – a thrill.

The only time the prisoners got a factory-made cigarette or a piece of candy was around Christmas through the kindness of a guard or official. Some prisoner-carpenters or painters that worked at a civilian's home were invariably handed a good smoke. Candy dishes within easy reach became empty.

Very few of the prisoners were church minded. Most of them were atheists, without the comforts of any belief. The rest had a faint attachment to some creed but were far from religious. There were some prisoners who were extremely religious and tried to convert their fellow prisoners. Chapel was held every Sunday for those who wished to attend. Attendance was not very good.

Men who had murdered and robbed ruthlessly were inclined to be godless. This accounted for the lack of interest in religion at Alcatraz. There was a chaplain on full-time duty. But most of his duties concerned the religious educational program. A San Francisco priest visited every Sunday and was highly regarded by the prisoners for his fatherly interest in them. He spent some time in the hospital with the patients and visited the other prisoners in the cellhouse or in the yard. He had impromptu talks with the prisoners, inquired as to their health and well being, and offered his help.

On the Jewish holidays, a rabbi held congregation for the Jewish prison population. They were allowed to fast during the Jewish New Year, as was the ritual. During the Feast of Passover, matzo was placed on the mess hall tables.

The one sure sign of the approaching Christmas holiday season was not the tang in the air or the appearance of magazine advertisements and pictures. It was the run on the dentist's office because of the anticipated turkey dinner.

"See that my teeth are in shape, will yuh, doc?" they pleaded.

Escape

All day the fog drifted in from the sea – tumbling, billowing clouds of it. It was as though nature laid a fleecy white smoke screen over San Francisco Bay. The fog was so thick you could almost reach out and make snowballs.

The timid ferries groped along like nearsighted old grandmas who had misplaced their glasses and to whom everything was a white blur. Devil-may-care tramp freighters usually wallowed cockily in and out of the Golden Gate but inched along cautiously now. The tiny blue craft of the Italian fisher folk nestled side-by-side at San Francisco's Fishermen's Wharf, waiting for the fog to rise before venturing out to sea.

And out from the white void that was the Bay came the din of foghorns. They screeched in agony or brayed raucously or shrieked like sirens. San Francisco newspapers, in huge headlines, called it the heaviest fog in twenty years. But later in the day those headlines were replaced by a more absorbing story – Alcatraz Escape.

Throughout the morning, the prisoners followed the regular work routine. Wisps of fog seeped in through the barred windows and everything outside resembled a gigantic, shapeless snow bank.

Following the noon meal, the men shuffled back to the workshops. At 1 p.m. they were checked in. Each man was accounted for. All was well.

In one portion of the shop building, where the blacksmith shop adjoined the mat shop, the prisoners worked methodically. Six prisoners were in the blacksmith shop, twenty-six in the mat shop. The blacksmith's ringing clang of striking metal blended with the thuds and hacking of the mat shop workers. The guard on duty saw that they were performing their work. He left to oversee workers in another side of the building.

Two men looked up from their work. One was in the mat shop and the other in the blacksmith shop. Watching the guard leave, they put down their tools. They ambled over to a window with its chunks of heavy criss-crossed glass and tool-proof steel.

Somewhat brazenly, one of them hauled out a hacksaw from his work shirt. As though sawing a piece of metal on his workbench, he started hacking the window's metal framework. First, he gouged out a bit of painted putty. It was concealing a deep gash in the steel that probably took weeks to file – weeks of patient work, of stolen moments, sawing away whenever the guard left the shop for brief intervals.

"There she comes," one of them grunted, as the framework snapped under one final, vicious thrust. They swiftly cut out a portion of heavy glass. And through the small porthole-like opening swirled the fog, heavy with the salty-tang of the sea. The two prisoners probably sniffed it eagerly. It was the air of freedom.

Meanwhile, the other prisoners kept at their tasks. They knew well enough what was going on by the window – their occasional interested glances proved it. But they gave not one cry of alarm.

The two prisoners turned from the window and faced the other prisoners. Good-byes were said silently, with gestures and a flourish of the hand. Then the smaller one of the two hoisted up to the narrow opening. Squirming and writhing like a human corkscrew, he forced himself through. His companion, taller and thinner, followed. For a few minutes it looked as though he were stuck. With a desperate twisting movement, he squeezed through.

Dropping to the ground, they crouched low against the wall and listened. The wool-thick fog swirled around them. There were no shouts of alarm, no frenzied blowing of guards' whistles. Only the regular noise was heard — the clamoring workshops, moaning foghorns, and swishing of icy Bay waters lashing against the Island.

Through white mist, they distinguished a guard patrolling the roof of a building opposite them. They realized one suspicious noise or a glimpse of their darting figures and they would be showered with machine gun bullets. Not daring to breathe, they crouched against the shop building. The guard, walking his post, passed out of sight.

Like racing whippets springing after a mechanical racetrack rabbit, they leaped up and sprinted swiftly toward a distant gate. It was through this gate that the useless bits of tires from the mat shop were dumped over the twenty-foot cliff. A padlock dangled on the gate. Prepared, one of the prisoners took a wrench from his trousers, twisted the lock until it snapped and swung the gate wide open.

They closed the gate, trotted to the edge of the cliff and went over the side. The cliff was almost perpendicular. Their fall was broken by the accumulation of discarded old tires below.

Most prisoners knew that the two men had made elaborate preparations for the break. A marathon swimmer contemplating conquering the English Channel couldn't have made more detailed preparations than these two.

For months they subjected themselves to icy, needlepoint cold showers. They smuggled gobs of gooey grease and numerous gallon tin cans from certain shops. The cans were carefully sealed and hidden near the gate.

On reaching the water's edge, they removed their prison garb, smeared their bodies with grease, and improvised an air raft from the sealed cans. Then they plunged into the chilly gray waters of the Bay and disappeared into the fog.

Back in the shop, there wasn't the slightest inkling that anything was wrong. The other prisoners whammed and hacked and slashed at their shop tasks with verve, hoping the pair would escape. A half-hour later, the guard returned. He ran his eyes down the printed checkup sheet that listed the number and task of every prisoner in his workshops.

He was missing two men! He recounted. Still there were two men missing – Ralph Roe and Theodore Cole. Prison officials were notified. The other prisoners in the shop were ordered to line up and were questioned.

"When did Roe and Cole disappear? How did they get away?"

The prisoners merely shrugged their shoulders, professing ignorance. Threats of harsh punishment or the dungeon itself couldn't have dragged any information from them. "We didn't see anything – we don't know nothing." It was the code of the underworld. Never "rat" or squeal on a pal. Never help the law by spilling your guts.

Officials made a cursory inspection of the shop. A gaping hole, the filed windowpane, twisted steel, and cut out glass mutely told the story. The deadly monotony was broken. Prisoners were bustled back to their cells. The escape siren screeched. Orders were barked. All guards were routed for immediate duty. Search parties were organized; searchlights and gas billys distributed. No one could leave the Island.

Prison officials surmised that Roe and Cole were hiding on the Island. They believed no man would take his chances in the turbulent, icy waters of the Bay that December day.

The tide was running fast. Northern California rivers that disgorge into San Francisco Bay were at flood levels. Incessant rains converted the rivers into seething, raging agents of destruction. Their dirty brown floodwaters gushed into the Bay, churning onward toward the Golden Gate and out to sea.

Driftwood bobbed and swirled dizzily in the Bay during such tide conditions. Human bodies would receive a similar buffeting ride. A few days before, a soldier fell off a launch that was en route to nearby Angel Island. Before the craft could be halted and a life preserver thrown, he was pulled away by the swift-running current and drowned.

Groups of guards examined the Island inch-by-inch. Every crevice, sewer and cave where a man could hide was searched. Flashlights played over these possible hideouts. Some underground holes were gassed. No cowering, coughing, crying prisoners came out – only wisps of gas.

When it became apparent that the prisoners took to the water, the search became more widespread. Frantic calls were made to Washington, the San Francisco police, the Coast Guard, and the Army. Almost immediately, Army planes took off from Crissy Field, roaring low over the Bay. Sleek gray Coast Guard cutters and the police boat David White started cruising toward the Island. Lookouts peered into the gray water hoping to spot the prisoners – but visibility was only a matter of feet because of the fog.

It was not until 3 p.m. that their aid was asked. This gave Cole and Roe approximately a two-hour lead in the fast water of the Bay. Alcatraz communicated constantly with the Coast Guard by radio during the search. Ferries and other craft were asked to be on the lookout. Coast Guard vessels crossed and re-crossed the water, ever enlarging their radius. Small craft were stopped and searched.

The warden informed the press of the escape. A launch carrying a group of venturesome reporters drew up to the Island. The tower guard fired a warning shot over their heads.

"Hey, cut it out – we're reporters – we're looking for the Coast Guard," one cried.

Wham – wham – two more shots came streaking out of the guard tower. They tried to steer away from the Island but the motor stalled. Once underway, the fog swallowed them.

The search for the escaped prisoners spread to San Francisco. A cordon of police stretched around the teeming Embarcadero waterfront. All small incoming craft were searched. That night Alcatraz officials received a tip that the prisoners might be hiding in a certain warehouse in San Francisco or in a freighter anchored in the Bay. The Alcatraz radio summoned a Coast Guard cutter. Six guards were mustered aboard and the cutter sped to the suspected warehouse and freighter. A labored search proved fruitless.

G-men joined in the search. Thousands of "Wanted" posters were distributed. G-men examined the Alcatraz files, hoping to get clues from the visitor or mail logs.

Orders were given by the Department of Justice to carry on the search until Roe and Cole were found – dead or alive. Alcatraz officials believed the men drowned and their bodies swept out to sea through the Golden Gate. On this assumption, a G-man was stationed atop the Golden Gate Bridge with binoculars. His job was to hunch over the rail and watch the water below for a body.

The morning after the escape, the prisoners were restless and uneasy. They were certain Cole and Roe made a clean getaway but did not know whether they obtained freedom or death in the Bay.

They soon accepted the theory that the two prisoners were alive and free, and a holiday spirit permeated the cellblock. Small outbreaks of joyous shouting and whistling occurred in the cells. The prisoners were jubilant that two of their own broke out of the escape-proof prison. They enlightened each other with lighthearted repartee.

"So this is maximum security."

"I guess I'll learn how to swim, too."

"Two of our buddies sure put it over on the Department of Justice!"

"If they're hiding out on the Island, they won't starve – they've got the warden's goat."

I approached a prisoner who was confined in the hospital and asked how he felt.

"I feel twenty years younger, doc. I feel better than the warden does this morning, I can bet you. Honest, doc, you don't know what that escape means to us cons. It gives us hope – puts new life into us. I mean the hope of escape. Some of us never do anything about it, except think of escape. But it whiles away the long hours. Without that we'd crack. I know what it is. I thought about it for eight years at San Quentin. I planned and planned but nothing happened. But it helped me endure the time."

"I imagine," I mused aloud, "you need good nerves to get out of a place like this."

"The place can't be made that can't be beaten by time and patience," the prisoner retorted.

"But it's questionable whether they made it. In all probability they were drowned. If they were, their bodies would be found floating out through the gate."

The prisoner shook his head.

"I think they made it, doc. It was all pretty well planned. They had something to keep them afloat – oil cans from the machine shop. I know a guy who broke out of San Quentin. They claimed they found his body in the Bay. Two years later I saw him in Mexico City."

"But the water was cold – they couldn't have stood it for long."

"They thought of that, too, doc. They took ice cold showers for a long time and plenty of exercise to toughen them. Hell, they had nothing to do but plan it for the two years they were here."

"Well, Roe has a little money on the outside and some contacts. If he made Frisco, he's safe. If they got to the other shore near Sausalito, they could head for Mt. Tamalpais. There are a thousand homes in them mountains. They could get all the food and clothing they need. It would take the whole U. S. Army to get them out of the hills."

Cole and Roe were soon the idols of the prisoners. Bank robbers, kidnappers, once notorious public enemies, and the small fry bad men on the Rock lionized the two escaped prisoners much as students would a football hero.

Roe, a tall well-built man, was serving 99 years for robbing the Farmer's National Bank at Sulphur, Oklahoma. He was sent to Alcatraz because of the long term. A handsome man with a disarming, friendly smile, he was the type who adapted to institutional life.

Two months before the escape, Roe spent nine days in the prison hospital with a minor stomach ailment. His condition, it appeared now, was doubtless a result of the mental and nervous strain under which he labored while planning the escape. On the third day of his hospital stay, he remarked to a fellow prisoner,

"Something went haywire." Doubtless he was referring to his escape.

"How are you getting along here?" I once asked him.

"Fine."

"Doesn't that 99 year sentence bother you?"

"No. I get along fine, doctor. I work during the day and have plenty of reading at night. It keeps me pretty active and busy and I don't have much time to think about it."

"It's quite a stretch."

"I intend to make the best of it and enjoy myself as much as I can. I'm not the type that worries. Anyway, who knows what the future may bring."

His condition did not necessitate his being in bed. He whiled away his hospital hours gazing out the window. It was apparent now that he wasn't just passing the time away. He was analyzing the incoming and outgoing tides, studying the water, and the craft that passed daily. One thing was certain. Although his stay in the hospital was advantageous from this point of view, he did not fake his way into the hospital. He was truly sick and actually lost weight.

On January 27, 1938, the escape was an event of the past. A routine inspection revealed some tampering on the bars in one of the hospital toilets. A hasty examination revealed that not much damage was done. But on closer inspection, it was apparent that not much more was necessary for an escape to be effective.

Prison officials were summoned to the scene. They examined the bars. Secretive, furtive glances were directed toward the hospital prisoners to determine the culprit.

The prisoners knew nothing. That was their code. But some of them did know.

"Sure, it was Roe that did it. He wasn't taking chances of his other escape plans blowing up," a prisoner whispered.

This toilet was at the back of the large ward in the hospital. The window overlooked a metal staircase fifteen feet below. A drop could easily have been made to this landing. For the next few days, an extra guard patrolled outside at night. Because of suspected trouble, the tower guards over the work area were also doubled.

On the morning of January 29, prison guards repaired the damage and welded the bars. It was then that they realized the seriousness of the situation. A bar of the tool-proof steel cage was sawed completely through on the bottom and half way through on the top. The bars were kept in place with putty and painted silver to escape detection.

A hospital patient could work in the toilet all night and saw the bars without being seen or heard. He could then return to his bed when counts were made. For the patient's convenience, a large pendulum clock told them just when the guard came up for count. When the guard was gone, he could get up again to finish his task.

He didn't worry about lack of sleep. Patients slept long hours during the morning and afternoon.

Then came the shakedown to search for the hacksaws. Turning the hospital and wards inside out proved futile. No instruments or blades were found.

The situation in the hospital changed. The doors of both toilets were removed. The prisoners no longer enjoyed any privacy in their toilet habits.

"I would like to take a bath," a prisoner said after that. "Can I have the screen to put in front of the bathroom?"

"Since when are you getting so naïve? Those doors were removed for a purpose. You will just have to bear up under the strain of being seen by the other men."

The guards and prison officials thought that an escape could not be affected in this manner. But the prisoners were of a different opinion.

"Sure, they could have made it," a prisoner once said to me.

"But how?"

"Easy enough. Three bed sheets – and there are ten beds to choose from – and he could have been down to the landing without a sound."

"But he was still on the Island."

"We have an answer for everything. At the bottom of the landing all he had to do was sneak around and hide by the side of the morgue and wait. We know just when the guard comes around on his patrol. He's armed, too. He could be overpowered and his clothes taken, with a gun to boot. From then on, dressed as a guard, and with a gun, the rest would be easy. He could slip off the Island from many points."

"That's a tough assignment."

"Sure it's tough. It takes a tough man to do it. And when a man has nothing to lose, he's goddam tough."

Cole was doing a fifty-year term for kidnapping. Agile and wiry, he was called a "greased pig" escape artist. He attempted to flee from other prisons – once by hiding in a laundry bag and cutting his way out with a self-made knife – and once by hiding in a garbage can. Cole – who was younger, smaller, and more impulsive than Roe – remarked to fellow prisoners at Alcatraz,

"Nobody is going to take the best fifteen years of my life. I'll get over that damn wall – guards, guns, and all."

Once a fellow prisoner pointed out a sewer and commented it was a "good place to hide out." On that very same day, the prison authorities cemented the hole. This enraged Cole. He threatened to kill the prisoner.

"You tip me off, then you tip off the warden," he ranted.

Through the influence of friends, he calmed down. They assured him it was merely a coincidence.

After their arrival at Alcatraz, Cole and Roe asked to be put on the plumbing gang. They were both refused because of their records. Their interest in the plumbing gang was obvious now. The plumbing gang wandered over the Island making necessary repairs. They knew every nook, corner and crevice, knowledge ideal to anyone planning an escape.

The escape was immortalized in song and story written by admiring fellow prisoners.

The Jail in Alcatraz Bay, Some Don't Like To Stay, began one song.

"Say, doc," a prisoner orderly said, "did you read the new book?"

"What book?"

"*Gone with the Tide* – it's 3.5. All the cons are buying it."

Another joke began,

"Did you hear Santa Claus is coming to visit us this year?"

"But he can't cross the Bay."

"He could make it with a couple of cans, like our boys did."

Gone With the Tide was written by a prisoner and convulsed the men for days. Copies were in great demand. It smacked of simple folk-song cowboy tunes and was a hero-worshipping saga.

Gone with the Tide

Now gather around you prisoners
Hear this story I have to tell,
Of how two boys left Alcatraz
This living, burning hell.

On the 16th day of December
With Christmas drawing nigh,
These boys bid for their liberty
And went out with the Tide.

The tide was running very fast
The fog was very low,
These boys left Devil's Island
Bound for old Frisco.

They tossed tow cans out in the Bay
With a parting look, a can each took,
As they went out with the tide.

These boys were very careful
In laying out their plans,
Why they even thought of dry clothes
And sealed them in these cans.

Our warden did not like it
But still he can't deny,
They did not use no rough stuff
They just went out with the Tide.

Now the boys that left this Island
Had plenty of guts, you know,

Just a couple of old smart prisoners,
Who? King Cole and Old Ralph Roe.

Someone has got to take the rap
I wonder who it will be,
Boat-foot Warden Johnston or our meat head
deputy?

Following the escape, the Department of Justice
announced that an investigation was under way to
strengthen Alcatraz and to prevent any future jail
breaks. There was much conjecture how this would
be accomplished. Precautions discussed included
keeping the prisoners in their cells during unusually
foggy days, charging the fence with electricity,
more rigid surveillance by guards, and installing
tool-proof steel to many other buildings.

The gate that Cole and Roe slipped through was
reinforced with barbed wire and closed off. Refuse
from the work area and rubber from the mat shop
was no longer disposed of through the gate. A roof
guard constantly surveyed the water's edge.

Authorities were fearful of another break. Some
prisoners knew the escape plan – and may have
helped the escapees. The assumption was that Cole
and Roe – if they were alive – were hiding at a
predetermined place and would probably attempt to
liberate those who helped them. A massive jailbreak
was something all prisoners dreamed about. If it
were being contemplated, how would it be done?
When would they strike?

REUNION IN ALCATRAZ

Alcatraz was a malevolent Shangri-La. It was as isolated as the fantastic mountain in the film *Lost Horizon*, where time stood still. Time also stood still in Alcatraz, as most prisoners were serving 90-year or lifetime sentences. Those who were released found themselves old and gray and wrinkled – like those who groped their way out of ageless Shangri-La.

Alcatraz isolation was the best medicine for modern, high-powered gangsters. While at Atlanta or Leavenworth, they remained in touch with their gangs, retained their far-reaching influence behind prison bars, had money, dope and guns smuggled to them, and often shot their way out of prison.

Alcatraz housed the cream of America's gangster crop. There were many strange reunions. Al Capone met his hated rival, Silent Jim Ryan of the Terrible Touhy gang. Alvin Karpis found his former partner in crime, Arthur "Doc" Barker.

Alcatraz officials, familiar with the personnel of former gangs, did not place two erstwhile gangster pals or two big-shot gangster rivals in the same workshop. In the mess hall, pals and rivals ate at widely separate tables. Their only opportunity for meeting was in the yard. Here the captains, lieutenants and satellites of the various gangs often congregated in cliques. Should one clique wander over and converse with another, the watchful guards broke it up.

Sometimes the long incarcerations caused rival gang leaders to end the hateful feuds. This was the case with Capone and Ryan. When Ryan first landed on the Rock, he called Capone a "big wop bully." Ryan never missed a chance to taunt Capone. Capone returned the animosity, contemptuously terming Ryan "common." He hated Ryan because he hated anyone connected with the Touhys, and he hated them because, as he once told me,

"After all I did for Touhy and his family, he turned against me. You know what I did for him? I got a 25-year detainer taken off his sentence and besides that, I gave his brother money and helped out his family."

Then Capone, his mind beginning to crack, was sent to the prison hospital where Ryan was an orderly. Capone, dazed and childish, forgot his hatred of Ryan. Ryan, toting Capone's meal trays and making up Capone's bed said, "Aw, you can't take it out on a guy who's going nuts. I haven't anything against Capone anymore." And so the Capone-Ryan feud ended.

Besides Ryan, two other members of the Terrible Touhy gang were on the Rock. They were Isaac Costner – a robbery specialist – and Ludwig "Dutch" Schmidt – a Chicago torpedo (bodyguard). This gang cut a swathe of murder, kidnapping and robbery through Chicago. They made a big mistake when they left their fingerprints on a beer bottle. This happened after Costner and Schmidt, plus "Ice Wagon" Connors and Basil Banghardt, robbed a

Charlotte, North Carolina mail truck in Hollywood crime-movie fashion.

The truck, carrying $105,000, swung down a side street in Charlotte. The driver saw a car blocking the road at almost right angles and brought the truck to a screeching halt. Before he realized what had happened, four men poked a submachine gun against his stomach and fled with a fortune in Reserve Notes. G-men had only two slim clues to work on: (1) the driver remembered that one of the men walked with a limp, and (2) the robbers used a car stolen from another state.

After the townspeople reported seeing scores of sinister strangers with a limp, police raided an apartment where a "limping man" was said to be living. They found beer bottles bearing four sets of fingerprints belonging to Costner, Schmidt, Connors, and Banghardt. The desperados were captured when the stolen car was found parked outside a swank Baltimore apartment house. Costner was sentenced to 30 years, Schmidt to 32 years.

On Alcatraz, Schmidt wielded a pick and shovel instead of a submachine gun. He was a laborer on the road gang. Costner worked in the prison renovating plant where employees sent their uniforms and civilian clothes to be cleaned, pressed, and mended.

The rest of the Touhy gang "got theirs" when they were fingered for the John Factor kidnapping. The four ringleaders were each given 99-year sentences.

Factor, known in the shady circles of England and America as Jake the Barber, was kidnapped in 1933 as a quaint underworld prank. In picking Jake as their victim, the Touhy's gambled that the Factor family would not call the police because Factor was wanted in England on stock fraud charges. British authorities clamored for Factor and G-men were called to produce him.

The underworld told G-men that dapper Factor was kidnapped as he rode home from an exclusive gambling casino. Factor was released eight days later after paying $50,000 ransom. He had been beaten, burned and blindfolded the entire time. Factor was not sure of his kidnapper's identity.

G-men suspected the Touhy gang and started working on this theory. But the gang vanished from their haunts. A search was fruitless. Then, in Wisconsin, fate played into the hands of the authorities. Four inebriated "fishermen" in an expensive car ostentatiously filled with fishing poles and tackle ran into a telephone pole. A police officer – about to arrest the quartet for drunken driving – looked into the rear of the car, spied a rifle, a flock of pistols, enough ammunition for a siege, and changed his mind. Roger Touhy, "Gloomy Gus" Schaefer, Willie Sharkey, and Eddie McFadden readily admitted their identity. They laughingly boasted the kidnapping charge would never stick. But it did stick and that was the end of the Touhy gang.

Roger Touhy, the commander-in-chief, was the son of a Chicago police officer. He and his five brothers grew up as hoodlums then graduated into the gangster class. Three brothers were killed in underworld shootings, one disappeared and the other two, including Roger, received long-term prison sentences.

All three leaders of the Urschel kidnapping gang – swaggering George "Machine Gun" Kelly, respectable Harvey Bailey and high-living Albert Bates – were reunited on Alcatraz. This brazen gang led the hounds of the law on an exhaustive chase from state to state, through an area totaling 683,000 miles. Intensive though the chase was, it was short. Within three months, 16 people were behind bars.

The drama began one July afternoon in 1933, when two of the gang members entered the home of Charles F. Urschel in Oklahoma City. Urschel, his wife and two friends, Mr. And Mrs. Walter Jarrett, were playing bridge.

"Which one is Urschel?" growled one of the gunmen, pointing a machine gun at the party while the other waved a pistol.

In frozen amazement, neither Urschel nor Jarrett replied. Both were hustled outside into an automobile from which Jarrett was promptly released. Four days later, they demanded $200,000 ransom. An intermediary was named and instructed to take a train to Kansas City. At a signal alongside the railroad track, he was to throw the money out the window. No signal appeared. The intermediary proceeded to the designated Kansas City hotel. Late that afternoon a voice over the telephone ordered him to go to such and such a hotel, and then walk west. He did. One of the kidnappers approached and relieved him of the money.

Urschel was returned after nine days, haggard and on the verge of collapse. G-men, who were impatiently holding off until Urschel was safely home, now swooped down on the trail. Urschel was blindfolded the entire time. He was able to tell what kind of a bed he slept on, how often it rained, and how long the trip to the hideout had taken. He recalled hearing cows, chickens and other farmyard noises at the place where he was held. And twice a day, an airplane flew overhead – at 9:45 a.m. and 5:45 p.m.

Checking all airplane schedules revealed that American Airways operated a line between Fort Worth and Amarillo, Texas. Further deduction revealed that a plane was in the vicinity of Paradise, Texas at the times specified by the victim. As files were combed for suspects, the names of "Machine Gun" Kelly and his wife, Kathryn, appeared. Investigation into Kelly's recent activities revealed the marriage of Kathryn's mother to a Robert Shannon, who lived on a ranch near Paradise! G-men raided the farmhouse just before dawn and found Bailey with large wads of ransom money in his pockets. One room in the house was an arsenal. Kelly's father-in-law and mother-in-law were taken into custody at the same time as Bailey.

Shortly afterwards, crafty Albert Bates was arrested in Denver. Bates was given $100,000 of the ransom money and maintained that someone put the finger on him. Gunmen, robber and jail-breaker, Bates started his crime career at 14 and never held a legitimate job in all his 43 years – because he said legitimate jobs never paid enough to procure him the high-powered cars, fine apartments, country club memberships and servants to which he had always been accustomed. On Alcatraz, where he was serving a life term, Bates had his first steady job. He dusted shelves, sorted books, and mended torn pages in the prison library. For recreation, he played handball and read adventure stories.

With Bailey and Bates behind bars, the search now concentrated on Kelly and his wife. During the trial of the other gang members, Kelly wrote threatening letters to Urschel and the U.S. Assistant Attorney General warning them to lay off his pals or he would make it hot for them. While at large, Kelly talked big, thumbed his nose at law officials, nonchalantly took long chances and, patting his machine gun, boasted he would never be taken alive. But when he and his wife were finally captured in Memphis, Kelly went docilely with the officers. His braggadocio collapsed like a balloon.

Kelly was serving a life sentence. His fingers, once nimble with a machine gun, were kept busy sorting sheets, shirts, socks and shorts in the prison laundry. Kathryn was sentenced to an Oklahoma jail for her part in the Urschel kidnapping.

Harvey Bailey, the third leader of the Urschel kidnappers, was another lifer on the Rock. Bailey, who also belonged to the Keating-Holden gang of bank robbers in St. Paul, had a respectable background. His father, a West Virginia farmer and cattleman, was a strict disciplinarian with his numerous offspring. He made sure that they attended Baptist Church regularly.

Bailey left home at 20 and was employed on the Illinois Central Railroad. In eight years, he worked himself up from laborer to fireman, and then to locomotive engineer.

Bailey's former boss said that he was industrious, neat, faithful, willing to work overtime, and respected by the other employees. Through a woman, Bailey became involved with a gang of bootleggers and dope peddlers. His boss, with Bailey's best interests at heart, told the young man to forget the girl and get some sleep at night. Bailey said, "It's none of your damn business," walked away and never returned to his job.

He was soon a bootlegger, making such rich profits that he was able to buy a $45,000 farm in Wisconsin and a $25,000 home. Then somebody pinned a bank robbery on him. Bailey said it was somebody who bore him a grudge. The charge was dismissed but Bailey blamed his subsequent crime career on the unnamed person who "did him dirt." Turning his farm and home over to his wife, Bailey fled the neighborhood and turned to criminal pursuits. In Wisconsin, many of Bailey's friends included some of the finest business people in the community. They still believed him innocent of his subsequent crimes.

Bailey was employed in the Alcatraz model shop where he made furniture.

When Francis Keating and Tommy Holden headed the St. Paul gang, Bailey was their gifted henchman. These two former Chicago boys were also reunited on Alcatraz.

St. Paul was a "good" town for mobsters and gunmen to live. So long as they didn't practice in the city limits, they were unmolested except for an occasional routine "pushing around" in a police station.

Between 1930 and 1931, Keating and Holden gathered a coterie of experienced gangsters. They lived in style – spending money in nightclubs and casinos and playing golf on the best courses. It was on a golf course six miles outside Kansas City that G-men tapped Keating and Holden on the shoulder for the last time. Bailey was with them but the agents didn't recognize him. He nonchalantly walked away from the group and was not apprehended until some time later.

Important lieutenants of the St. Paul gang were cold-blooded Verne Miller, once a South Dakota sheriff and later a Capone torpedo, and his pal, bald-headed Frank Nash, bank robber, murderer and prison breaker. In 1933, Miller directed the diabolical Kansas City massacre at Union Station. Here his friend Nash was unintentionally killed while G-men were transferring him from a train to a car. Four agents were also killed. The underworld never forgave Miller for the botched job. He was finally rubbed out by his own kind; his horribly mangled body was tossed into a marsh in another state.

The St. Paul gang blazed a bloody trail of mail, payroll and bank robberies throughout the Midwest. Once, while robbing the Kraft State Bank at Menomonee, Wisconsin, the gang kidnapped the son of the bank president and held him as a shield during the furious and subsequent chase. During the flight, two gang underlings murdered the president's son and for this mistake were killed themselves later by gang bosses.

The job that put Keating and Holden behind bars was the $150,000 armed robbery of a mail train in Illinois. The cash was never recovered. Once caught, they received long sentences and were sent to Leavenworth. After 22 months, they escaped by forging two passes. For two years they were on the "lam," boldly spending most of their time close to Leavenworth – where they calculated officers were least likely to look for them. A tip sent G-men to the golf course outside Kansas City and that was the temporary end of the Keating-Holden gang.

Keating maintained he was framed on the mail robbery rap.

"They had to get somebody to keep the slate clean and they thought I was a good candidate," he complained to prison officials.

Keating was eligible for parole in a few years. "But I won't make it," he said. "They will ask me where the money is. I'll tell them I am innocent and don't know where it is. The answer will be 'you don't want a parole. You want a pardon.' So I guess I'll be here a long time yet." Keating was an ardent prison baseball player. In the summer of 1937, he fractured his left leg while sliding into a base.

Keating's job on Alcatraz was sorting laundry. Holden, who hated cops all his life, served meals to the prison guards and other members of the prison staff in the officer's mess hall.

The Keating-Holden gang was soon revived under the able leadership of two other crime professors, "Doc" Barker and Alvin Karpis, along with Charles "Big Fitz" Fitzgerald, Harry Campbell, and the renegade Volney Davis. All these big shots were lifers on Alcatraz.

Davis split with the gang after the Bremer kidnapping because hatchet-faced Ma Barker didn't like his current gun moll (girlfriend). One of the gang met Davis in a restaurant, gave him $500 and snarled, "You're lucky you're getting off this easy. Now scram and if we ever see your mug again it'll be curtains for you." But a few months later, Davis was under the same restraining roof with his old gang, former grievances forgotten in their common woes.

Frank Nash introduced Karpis and Barker to Keating and Holden in St. Paul. High strung, youthful Alvin Karpis was better known as "Old Creepy" because of his tight-lipped, cold-blooded snaky aspect. Sleek, diminutive and vicious, Barker was a murderer at 22. Waiting until Keating and Holden were safely in prison, the ex-prisoners Karpis and Barker restored the disintegrating St. Paul gang to the big time. In 1934, they pulled their biggest job – the kidnapping of the wealthy banker and brewer, Edward George Bremer. It happened right in St. Paul, too, violating all gangland traditions that St. Paul must be kept a "good" town.

Returning from driving his child to school one morning, Bremer stopped for a traffic signal. Several men stepped on the running board of his car. One of them struck Bremer over the head. The bloodstained car was later found abandoned in a remote section of the city. A note was placed in a milk bottle and hurled through the glass door of a friend's home. It announced that the kidnappers wanted $200,000 ransom. The money was delivered and Bremer was released near Rochester, Minnesota. He was dropped there from a car after a long journey and forced to wear goggles painted black on the inside.

Bremer didn't know where he was held or any knowledge of his abductors. Neither did the authorities. But Bremer remembered that during the journey to Rochester, the kidnappers carried five-gallon tins of gasoline and tossed the empties on the highway. This precluded gas station stops and being scrutinized by an attendant. G-men found one of the empty tins not far from Rochester – and on it was the telltale smudge of a fingerprint. It turned out to be that of Barker. Now the authorities knew the culprits.

Karpis and Barker carried out the kidnapping but the brains were "Shotgun" George Ziegler, who matriculated from the old St. Paul gang, and Mrs. Kate "Ma" Barker. She was the 50-year-old gray-haired queen of the Barker-Karpis gang.

Ma, a gun-toting vixen, was a hardened criminal and the mother of three criminal sons. Two sons, Lloyd and Arthur, were long-term prisoners; the third, Fred, was killed in a machine gun battle with G-men.

Ma could handle a machine gun as dexterously as her boys and died with one in her hand. Anybody who didn't like what she said could tell it to her boys who were fiercely loyal to her. It was she who planned the bank robberies her boys pulled and it was she who gave or withheld the okay on the women of the mob.

When the gang learned that Barker's fingerprints were discovered on the gasoline can, they decided St. Paul was becoming too hot for them. They split up and traveled throughout the U.S. Some went to Havana, where wads of the kidnapping money was passed in the glittering white casinos.

Shotgun Ziegler was one of Capone's triggermen. He was also a master bank cracker. It was said he took part in the St. Valentine's Day massacre, which wiped out the Bugs Moran gang. Ziegler started talking too much. Some said that old Shotgun's mind was beginning to crack and that he boasted openly about the Bremer kidnapping. One day as he walked out of a Chicago café, four machine guns chattered, and that was the end of Ziegler.

His murder gave G-men an ace in the Bremer investigation. His apartment was discovered and valuable clues to the whereabouts of Barker and Karpis were found as well as the identity of other gang members. With the law drawing closer on their trail, the gang traveled faster. Nerves became frayed and they started quarreling. It was at this stage that Volney Davis withdrew.

At last it was learned that Barker and a confederate, "Slim" Gray, circled back to Chicago. An underworld finger pointed out the women the two were living with. The women were trailed to two north side apartments. One night an agent whistled up the speaking tube, "The place is surrounded, Barker. You'd better come quietly." Some of the gang came out with their hands up. Gray tried to run, shot at a G-man, and fell with a bullet through his bulletproof vest – and his heart. Barker was taken the same night as he walked out of the other apartment, unaware of what had happened to Gray.

In the latter's apartment, agents discovered a map of Florida with a circle drawn around Ocala. Sure enough, Ma and Fred Barker were discovered living in a large house on a bayou. Roads were blocked off and machine guns set up. "Come out, Mrs. Barker, and you too, Fred," a G-man shouted. "You're trapped." The answer was the coughing of a machine gun. The gun battle lasted for hours and when it was over, both Ma and Fred were dead.

Karpis and Campbell were traced to an Atlantic City hotel. When local police knocked on the door of their room, Karpis came out. He offered to step inside and get Campbell. Both came out with sputtering guns and escaped in the ensuing melee.

Now Karpis was labeled "Public Enemy No. 1" by screaming newspaper headlines. Throughout the land, small boys playing with toy guns pretended to be Karpis rather than Dillinger or Baby Face Nelson. At last, Karpis was caught in New Orleans, while Campbell was taken in Toledo.

The capture of Davis was perhaps the most spectacular of all. He was arrested in Kansas City and placed on a Chicago-bound plane. During a forced landing, the agent to whom Davis was handcuffed went into a tavern. Davis begged for a glass of beer and the agent uncuffed his prisoner. Suddenly Davis tossed the beer into the agent's face and dove out a window.

Several months later he was recaptured outside a Chicago house. The address was found on Davis when he was first captured. Agents had been watching the place for months. Finally, Davis was seen entering the house. In half an hour, the house was surrounded. Because they knew Davis was a desperate criminal and would inevitably shoot it out, the agents decided to wait until Davis came out to his car. After twenty minutes, Davis strolled down the walk. At the door of his car, the agents pounced on him. Davis struggled furiously. He tried to reach a .380 pistol in his car but was overpowered and reached Alcatraz without escaping again.

After his capture, Davis confessed to seizing countless slot machines. "I'd stick up a roadside place and walk off with a slot machine whenever I ran out of money. Some of them netted me $400."

All his life Davis was cursed with a twitchy restlessness that often caused him to jump into his car in the middle of the night and drive miles into nowhere. He found the confining life of the Rock harder to stomach than his pals. In his cell, he spent most of his time pacing back and forth. His job was one of the most monotonous – washing endless stacks of dishes, day after day after day in the prison kitchen.

Barker, whose prison intelligence test rated him far below normal despite his criminal wiliness, worked in the prison tailor shop with forty other prisoners. His pal Karpis had a job in the mat shop. Hostile and nervous Karpis would fight other prisoners at the drop of a handkerchief. Twice he did time in Alcatraz dungeons for letting his fists fly. Campbell also worked in the prison mat shop. Fitgerald was a cellhouse orderly.

There was one Alcatraz prisoner who was terrified of a reunion. Earl Phipps gaped in terror at each new arrival; beads of sweat moistened his face. He prayed the new prisoner wouldn't be Joe White or Forrest Holliday. They were the partners he "ratted on" when all of them were convicted for the Fargo National Bank robbery in North Dakota.

Phipps feared their vengeance. When the grapevine spread the word that a newcomer was arriving, Phipps spent sleepless nights, wide-eyed and jittery. Other convicts made brash overtures to new arrivals. But not Phipps. He lurked in the background, cap pulled low over his face, collar turned high, and glanced with apprehension at the new prisoner.

The haunting fear that some day, SOME DAY, the men he double-crossed would be transferred to the Rock preyed on his mind. The strain was terrific. Huddled in a corner of the yard, or at work in one of the prison shops, he twitched nervously when anyone approached him. Then one day Phipps complained there were snakes in his cell.

"They're writhing on the floor – when I walk, I squish them – they're thick on the walls – they're dangling from the bars – I don't know where they're coming from," he gasped.

He was kept in a hospital cell for mental observation and diagnosed as a dementia praecox (schizophrenic). We often wondered if he was faking the continual anticipation of his partners' arrival.

Then one day Forrest Holliday was transferred to Alcatraz from McNeil's Island Penitentiary. Prison officials ordered that both men be kept apart. Phipps squealed with fright in his hospital cell when he learned of Holliday's transfer.

"Don't open my door, doctor," he begged. "He'll try to get me – he'll kill me if he ever gets up here. He'll throw lye in my face. It'll eat my eyes out. Or he'll jam it down my throat or put it in my food. Or he'll throw a shiv at me."

For days, Phipps refused to eat unless it was handed to him by one of the guard attendants. In desperation, Phipps sought a deal and bribed a hospital official for a transfer.

"I want to speak to you in private – not right here – I want to go where we can't be heard," he whispered.

"You can say whatever you want right here," he was told.

"Okay. How would you like to find a package of money in your mailbox?"

"Just what do you mean?"

"I have friends outside. If you help me get a transfer to Springfield in ten days, I'll see that you get five thousand dollars."

"I'll have nothing to do with your transfer," the hospital official said. "Get back into your trance."

This incident was reported in a formal letter to the chief medical officer and placed in Phipps' record.

Phipps had a long prison history, with arrests for robbery and burglary, Army desertion, and grand larceny. Then came the bank robbery.

Originally sentenced to twenty years for the bank robbery, Phipps began his time at Leavenworth in 1936. He was transferred to Alcatraz the following year because of his incorrigible and vicious tendencies. The horror of being knifed or poisoned by the men he squealed on was a type of punishment not to be found in any penal code.

After days in the hospital cowering under a blanket and screaming for protection against Holliday, the psychiatrists from the transfer board examined Phipps. They recommended his transfer to the mental institution in Springfield.

KEEPER OF THE FAITH

There was one man on Alcatraz who did not understand the methods of modern gangs. He was aging Phil Ryan, also known as "Mike" and "Red." He was the Rock's grand old man, counselor to the newcomers, and keeper of the faith. Prisoners said he never squealed, either on pal or enemy.

Cracking safes and robbing the mails with an old-style Colt was Red's profession in the days when he was more agile. He practiced his art from Newport to Singapore. Red shook his head sadly over machine guns, ransom notes, baby snatchings and other adjuncts of present-day crime.

"Being a yegg (safecracker) was a profession, not a racket that any kid without any brains could get into," he complained to me. "We were yeggs because we liked adventure. We slept in the hills, in the cold and rain – not in fancy apartments. When we pulled a job, we planned it for weeks, down to every detail, so that nobody would get hurt. Sure, I used a gun, but I never killed anybody with it. Today they don't care who they kill. It's these dumb kidnappers and nit-wit bank robbers who spoiled the business for the rest of us by pulling the agents into the chase."

Red spent nearly half of his 70 years behind the bars of one prison or another. When he was released from a ten-year stretch in San Quentin, he found times – and safes – had changed. No longer could a yegg slip into an office with a mask and blowtorch. Locks on safes were so improved that nothing short of a stick of dynamite or a dangerous chemical could move them.

Red tried cracking a few of the new safes, but found his old tools unequal to the task. That hurt his professional pride. Pickings were slim. So he capitulated to the times and robbed the airmail at the San Francisco Presidio. He was caught and sentenced to 25 years. Three other men who helped Red were "out on the street" because Red declined to squeal and took the entire rap.

"No use everybody going to jail," he remarked. "Besides, I'm old and my friends are young with their lives before them."

Red was no convert to righteousness. He didn't tell the fish (newcomers) to go straight. But he did advise them against killing and kidnapping.

"Crack a safe and make a haul," he said. "But stay away from women and children. Stay away from the homes where they live. Go to offices and places of business. You're a man – all right, pick on a man."

Red suffered from a chronic ailment and, although he spent most of his time in the prison hospital, he still retained his influence among the prisoners. When they wanted counsel, they went to Red – old and wise in the way of prisons.

During the strike, he sent word to another prisoner in the isolation ward, "Tell Charlie old Mike said to get out of isolation and go back to work. The backbone of the strike is broken."

When Waley lay on a hospital cot, retching and sick from forced feeding, Red shuffled over to him.

"You won't get anywhere acting like that Waley," Red remarked kindly to the pariah. Red was probably the only prisoner who had spoken a civil word to the baby kidnapper for months. "Better eat a little something. No use being stubborn about it."

"I've made up my mind," grunted Waley. "I'm going out of here one way or another."

"Christ Waley, you'll ruin your stomach from that tube feeding," railed Red. "Then you'll always be sick. You're just a young kid and you'll have to live with your stomach an awful long time. You don't know what you're bucking up against."

"That's just it, Red. I have a whole lot of time to do and I can't do it here."

"You can do it, Waley. You're young and strong. Look at me. I was no youngster when I started doing this 25-year rap. I'll be past 80 if I ever get out. Now go on and eat something."

Waley promised to think it over and he finally followed Ryan's advice.

A solitary prisoner uses a heavy roller in the recreation yard. Notice the guard patrolling on the tower platform.

CAPONE

A drab cell replaced his lavish gang headquarters. Gray prison coveralls replaced delicately tinted silk underwear and fashionable suits. Hamburger loaf and hash replaced prepared dishes that intrigued Alphonse Capone, the epicure.

Yet Capone was still a big shot, even behind the wind swept walls of Alcatraz. He was still treated with respect by the other prisoners as well as the prison officials and still had his bodyguards. In the days when machine guns clattered like noisy typewriters in the streets of Chicago, 18 torpedoes flanked Capone. They surrounded him like the retinue of a wealthy Maharajah. On the Rock he had four "lobby-gobs." They constantly hovered near him whenever he mingled with the other prisoners in the yard.

Alcatraz was essentially for incorrigibles. Capone was not one of those. He was transferred to Alcatraz because of the publicity he received in the Atlanta prison. Newspapers ballyhooed the so-called good time he was having there; of how Atlanta had a commissary where prisoners could spend so much money a month and how Capone, who had a fabulous fortune, was "paying" other prisoners for favors.

Money was valueless on the Rock. A prisoner's personal belongings – including money – was locked up until his sentence was terminated. Besides, there was no commissary to purchase candy or cookies like in other prisons. Such delicacies were forbidden in Alcatraz.

Capone's transfer in August 1934 came as a jolting shock. One night, guards entered his Atlanta cell and awakened him. They commanded him to dress. He protested. Demanding an answer, he was informed that he was transferring to another institution. Capone, usually as passive as a stone Buddha, was indignant and seethed with rage as the guards shackled him.

He was herded into a barred railroad coach that was shunted on a siding. It was one of the railroad cars that transported him and fifty-one other criminals to the newly established penitentiary in San Francisco Bay.

And so Capone had another milestone in his hectic career – a milestone that read,

"Alcatraz, landing forbidden. Only government boats permitted. Others must keep away 300 yards. No one allowed ashore without a pass."

The barge bearing the coach pulled alongside the dock and two by two, like two-legged cargo trudging off an ark, Capone and the others set foot on the Rock. They eyed the husky, athletic guards in blue uniforms with unease. Methodically, the prisoners were searched. Capone writhed as a guard explored his hair, seams, shoes, pockets, and body cavities then inserted a pair of tweezers in his ears. The search failed to unearth any contraband, drugs or thin files.

Capone and the others observed the mechanical snitch with interest. It was the first time they saw a device that could detect metal. Then the prisoners were placed in a closed van and driven up the hill to the prison.

Once assigned to his cell, Capone peered out the barred window and saw the fog billowing in from the Golden Gate. He saw the Coast Guard cutters that convoyed the barge disappear into the mist. All about him was gray sloshing water.

Capone soon adapted to the harsh Alcatraz routine, becoming one of its model prisoners. At first, the other prisoners treated him with suspicion for they knew he had only a few more years to serve, while most of them would spend the rest of their lives there. Besides, they envied his fortune.

His amiable manner and eagerness to be on friendly terms with them soon dissipated most of this antagonism. But during those first few months their hatred of him culminated in numerous fights. His fellow prisoners regarded Capone as a "greaseball" – a flabby hulk with a rabbit's heart. They heckled him, jeered him, jabbed at him. In the fights that ensued, they discovered he could handle his dukes (fists).

The most serious fight was between him and Jimmy Lucas, a Texas bank robber. Lucas was getting a haircut in the basement barbershop. He watched Capone doing his janitorial work from the barber chair. Suddenly, Lucas reached for a pair of scissors and darted toward the unsuspecting Capone, whose back was turned. Lucas jabbed the scissors into Capone's back. Like a bull that felt the matador's blade, Capone bellowed and staggered away.

Lucas was upon him again, wielding the scissors. The blade sunk into Capone's hand. Capone sent Lucas sprawling. The three scars on Capone's face became red welts from rage. Capone started pummeling Lucas around the room. Reaching for his beloved mandolin-banjo, Capone smashed it on Lucas' head. Lucas collapsed in a heap. A half-inch piece of the scissors blade broke off and imbedded itself in Capone's left thumb. His thumb was operated on the same day and the blade was removed.

Whether it was his influence or that he would be safer and less molested, Capone was ultimately assigned to work in the yard. This was one of the easiest and most treasured jobs on the Rock. His duties consisted of keeping the yard in good condition. It was outdoor work and he could be by himself. Capone later confided the job made a new man of him – the exercise, sun and fresh air were responsible, he said.

Daily, he would strip to the waist and start pulling a 300-pound iron roller around, flattening out the baseball diamond. He dragged long, heavy planks across the earth to flatten it out or swept and raked up other parts of the yard. Other times he wielded a pick and shovel to dig up the earth at home plate and tamp it down again so it wouldn't be too dusty. Or sometimes he watered the entire enclosure with a hose.

Capone came to Alcatraz a pudgy, flabby hulk, weighing 240 pounds. The hard manual labor in the yard sweated fifty pounds off him and he became a well-built, husky man of 190 pounds. When I asked why he had been so stout and carried about so much weight, he replied,

"Well, I didn't have any time for anything. I didn't exercise. I spent most of my time in the hotel taking care of business. I hardly got out at all."

Capone was born in Brooklyn, New York on January 18, 1899 – the fourth of nine children. His father learned the barbering profession, married, and immigrated to New York from Italy. In Brooklyn, he operated a combination poolroom, bowling alley and barbershop.

The Department of Justice attempted to prove Capone was born in Italy but never could. Capone got as far as the sixth grade. He was fourteen and compelled to quit school to help support his family. Work was not new to him. He had been a pin boy (reset bowling pins) after school since he was twelve.

His first real job was in a box factory. For seven monotonous years, he punched a time clock. By doing this dull, uninteresting work, Capone rose from an unskilled beginner, earning seven dollars a week, to a skilled hand, making twenty-three dollars a week. In succeeding months, he managed dance halls in New York and Chicago, beaming at the customers, telling the dance bands how they should play and stepping in to halt free-for-all brawls.

The notorious Five Points gang was flourishing in New York and Capone slugged his way into its membership. It was there that he received three slashes across his face and the nickname Scarface. This won him gangland distinction. Twice he was involved in murder investigations by New York police. By 1920, he convinced the other Five Pointers that he had a facile trigger finger and knew how to use his ham-like fists.

Then Chicago's Johnnie Torrio wagged a beckoning finger and Capone responded. Torrio was the idol of the Five Points mob. Himself a Five Points product, Torrio went to Chicago and bludgeoned his way into a job as bodyguard for Big Jim Colosimo, the vice-dictator. Capone gulped at Torrio's invitation. Torrio – the personification of criminal success and flashy living – asked him – Al Capone – to come to Chicago!

Capone shed his baggy, shiny clothes for flashy ensembles. They DID things in Chicago. He accepted Torrio's invitation with devout thanks. Torrio installed him as a bouncer in the tough Four Deuces Café. To make it look more dignified, Capone was established next door to the Four Deuces. His business cards read "second-hand furniture dealer." Torrio's young protégé preened himself at the Four Deuces. It was reminiscent of San Francisco's former rootin'-tootin' Barbary Coast.

Twelve unsolved murders were staged there and Chicago's toughest gorillas, torpedoes, and hoodlums lazed about. Capone became familiar with them, including a one-time safe blower and burglar, Joe Howard. Howard was considered small potatoes, basking in the reflected glory of the other hoodlums. Then one day Howard attempted to hijack some Torrio liquor and was thrown a "handful of clouds" – murdered – near the Four Deuces.

The police sought Capone as one of the killers. The dragnet was out for him but he was nowhere to be found. Thirty days later, he walked into police headquarters, smiled and asked innocently if they were looking for him, and "was it anything important." He was bluntly informed that it was of very little consequence, "just a little case of murder." But he was released and beat the rap.

Torrio and his young protégé spent the next three years building their underworld combine – three dark and bloody years in which competitors and double-crossers were disciplined by elimination; three years that witnessed 135 gang murders. Cicero (near Chicago) became Capone territory and was thrown open to Capone gambling interests. Agents estimated Capone and Torrio were netting close to $100,000 a week. Dion O'Banion, florist by day and beer runner by night, loomed as a serious competitor. He was slapped down with a handful of clouds amidst the carnations in his flower shop.

During those years, Capone diced with death. There was a standing offer of $50,000 to any gunman who rubbed him out. He was trapped in several machine gun ambushes but escaped each time, unscathed. The most outstanding incident occurred in a Chicago hotel. He had just sauntered in and paused to chat with friends when two sedans pulled up to the curb. Out sputtered hundreds of machine gun bullets. At the first staccato rat-tat-tat, Capone plopped to the floor. Woodwork splintered about him, glass windows crashed, but he was unhurt.

Meanwhile, the government was prying into Capone's mysterious income, hammering at his breweries, and accumulating evidence. Unlike the other public enemies, Capone remained immune until the government moved against him. Investigators discovered Capone kept neither bank account nor books and never signed his name to checks. In 1932, he was sentenced to ten years for income tax evasion. The sum amounted to $140,885 over a three-year period. He was fined $30,000.

Asked how many times he was arrested during his career, Capone declared the arrests were too numerous to remember. He was arrested eight different times in Miami – all within twenty-four hours!

Capone was eligible for parole in 1935 but it was denied. Although his full term would expire in 1942, he accumulated 1200 days off for good behavior and was eligible to leave Alcatraz in 1939.

During his exile on the Rock, much happened to the world Capone once knew. G-men silenced guns and battled crime with laboratories and far-flung resources. Some cities named their own prosecutors in a drive against vice and crime. Most of his former powerful friends were rubbed out by gang guns or died of natural causes.

Frankie Rio had been Capone's number one bodyguard. Capone got the news at Alcatraz through the grapevine. It was just a terse "Frankie Rio's dead. His ticker jammed." This meant he died of a heart attack. Capone felt glum upon hearing this because he and Rio were the best of friends. Then there was "Machine Gun" Jack McGurn, also close to Capone. McGurn "got his" in a bowling alley on Chicago's northwest side, scene of the many shoot-down and drag-out gang wars in which McGurn won the title of being Capone's number one assassin.

Capone envisioned a life of ease when he completed his time. He mentioned an estate in Italy and planned to take a trip there, where he could loll in the sun and take long walks. On returning to America, he would retire to his palatial Florida estate, content with his already accumulated wealth, his wife and son, and turn philanthropist.

Capone's wealth was felt, even in Alcatraz. Although the prisoners had no money to spend inside the walls – and Capone could not bestow any sums on them for favors or gifts – it was well known that Capone supported many an Alcatraz prisoner's family. He interpreted this as charity, saying he felt sorry for them. Doubtless that was the way he obtained the service of his lobby-gobs.

It was Capone's money that was responsible for the Alcatraz band. An ardent music lover, he went starry-eyed when playing his mandolin-banjo. Capone contributed most of the instruments to the band. He offered to buy them outright but this was not allowed. He got around this by buying the instruments for himself and lending them to the other prisoners.

The band was one of his delights. Daily, after the noon meal, he sauntered to band practice, a portfolio of music tucked under one arm, his mandolin-banjo under the other. His shiny, expensive instrument was the "tenor of the string family." He explained that "it has eight strings and that's why I have to transpose my own music for it – the average music sheets are only arranged for four strings." He whiled away the long evening hours in his cell making these transpositions. Pudgy fingers clutching a pencil, he scrawled thick black notes on lined paper, oblivious to his surroundings.

Band practice was held in the basement. The other prisoners ambled in, toting their instruments. It was amusing to watch them practice. Each man wandered over to a secluded part of the room, ignored the others, and began playing his instrument. Invariably they played different selections. A trumpet player gave out hot-licks in swingtime, while a few feet away, a tuba player was compa-oompaing *Asleep in the Deep*. Near him a saxophonist was wheedling out the sentimental strains of *Might Lak a Rose*.

Standing like a troubadour of old, with his eyes half-closed in dreamy reflection, his legs spread apart, Capone strummed away on his mandolin-banjo, as though he was serenading under a lovely lady's balcony. His favorite tune was *Dark Eyes*. He played it over and over, his fingers briskly strumming and stroking the strings like fast-moving fat tarantulas.

Sometimes the band played a concert. Their concert hall was the cellblock. The instruments, including the piano, were carried to the east end of the cellblock after the noon meal. The prisoners crowded around, even occupying the upper two tiers to listen. The orchestra rendered several selections and the other prisoners applauded enthusiastically.

For several months, however, the band was suspended due to a lack of harmony. One afternoon, while the players practiced, some of the musician-prisoners took offense at some of the other's efforts. Saxophones, trumpets, clarinets and other instruments were wielded like clubs, thwacked down on heads. Then fists were used. Guards poured in and the melee ended.

Capone steadfastly refused to join any of the Alcatraz strikes or free-for-alls. The other prisoners spat out words to him like "yellow scab – fink – rat." Capone ignored them. He knew that with good behavior he would be out of Alcatraz in a short time. He explained to me once,

"I got my own skin to think of. Those other guys are here for life. Me, I gotta behave. I can't antagonize the administration." And he continued being a model prisoner, uncomplaining and ever willing to ingratiate himself with the prison officials.

The respect with which the officials treated Capone was evidenced in February 1938 when Capone suddenly cracked up. Once again he was the big shot. Prison officials lavished attention on him that no other prisoner ever had or doubtless would ever have. Capone "blew his top" with tragic suddenness. His lobby-gobs suspected something because they later admitted he acted queerly toward them. Numerous times, as they hovered near him in the yard, he spat at them – butted them in the pants with his knee and whispered, "Get the hell out of here."

Then early one weekday morning, Capone arose and donned his blue Sunday and holiday uniform instead of his gray, weekday garb. The cell doors clanged open for breakfast. The other prisoners stepped out of their cells and lined up to march into the mess hall – all save Capone. Guards found him sitting on the edge of his bunk, staring blankly at the floor.

"What's the matter, Al, don't you feel good?" a guard asked.

If this was any other prisoner, he would have been asked tersely just who the hell he thought he was, all dolled up in his Sunday clothes and refusing to march to breakfast. But he was still the big shot and still treated with deference. Capone replied in a daze,

"I guess I'm all right. I just don't want any breakfast."

"Have something anyway – how about some piping hot coffee?" the guard asked solicitously.

Capone wagged his head and muttered,

"Sure. That's a good idea. Sure. I think I'll go in and have some."

He trudged to the mess hall, sipped his coffee listlessly and returned with the line of other prisoners to the cellhouse. He appeared bewildered, groping his way weakly up the cellblock steps to the third tier. Unable to find his own cell, he wandered aimlessly about the tier. A guard came to his aid and led him back to his cell. The deputy warden was hastily called.

"What's wrong?" he asked.

Capone stared at him blankly.

"Nothing, deputy," he mumbled. "Nothing ..."

Capone fell forward on his face in a coma. Removed to the hospital, he came to and was placed in one of the mental observation cells called "nut cages" by the prisoners. He offered no resistance. In adjoining cells were Harmon Waley, the baby snatcher, and Harold June, who had delusions he was a gorilla.

"Whuz it all about?" Capone mumbled, as though he had a thick beefy tongue in his mouth. "I'll do anything you wan' me to do. Hones' I will."

He spent the first day in the hospital – as he did in succeeding days – confused, doing childish things. He made and re-made his bed, yanking off the blankets, throwing them back on the bed again, straightening them out, patting them affectionately.

As further evidence of Capone's importance, prison officials called in a San Francisco psychiatrist the next day – a Sunday! The officials continually asked the prison doctors how he was getting along.

"Why is he in the cage?" one official demanded. "Can't he be put out in the ward with the other men?"

Other officials interviewed Capone in the privacy of his cell numerous times, locking the door behind them. Their interest in Capone was amazing. Alcatraz prisoners were considered equal, to be treated fairly, with no special favors. Their egos were to be deflated by exile to Alcatraz. Names in headlines and high-ranking public enemies were to be just numbers. Yet Capone was still the big shot, rating attention no other prisoner received.

Most of the time Capone was in an elation jag, punctuating his childish antics with constant hearty language. He was so confused that he sometimes had hallucinations of varied sorts. Once during mealtime, I walked up to him and inquired how he was feeling.

"Fine, Doc, fine," he chuckled. "And you're looking swell yourself."

He reached out and grabbed my arm. It felt as though it was in a vice, for Capone was strong.

"What's the matter?" he asked. "Don't try to get away. I won't hurt you. Cool off. Am I hurting you? Is anything wrong? Tell Al."

Rather than let Capone's antics go farther, I sought to release myself from his fierce grasp. To attempt to jerk away would arouse him and cause a scuffle. So I decided discretion was wiser and started cajoling him.

"Everything's fine, Al," I said in a soothing tone. "Drink that hot coffee, Al. It will do you good. That's it, Al."

Capone stared at me with a demoniac expression.

"Do you think I should, Doc? All right then. But come back soon, huh?"

His talon-like fingers released their grip.

On the third day of his collapse, Capone awakened the other hospital prisoners around 4:30 a.m. by bellowing arias from Italian operas. His voice boomed through the corridors. Guards found him sitting up in bed, gesturing like an opera singer.

"Stop the singing, Al. It's early. All the other men are sleeping."

With a grand flourish, Capone beamed,

"Ah, but this is good music. They will like it."

And he burst into the drinking song from *La Traviata*, singing at the top of his voice,

Libiamo, libiamo, ne' lieti calici ….

Additional guards were summoned from the cellhouse. They pleaded with him to "pipe down, Al." But he did not understand. His voice soared on. Then he paused, saying,

"The music is good for the other boys in here. I'm cheering them up."

He became unruly and boisterous, swinging his arms as though they were windmill blades whirring around in a windstorm. Fearful that he might become violent, the guards entered his cell. To their surprise, he offered no resistance. Capone was taken from the "cage" and walked down the corridor to a special room. Laughing and singing, he was put to bed like a child and bound to it with a restraining jacket. He soon tired of singing. His voice grew hoarse. And, exhausted from his grandiose performance, he fell into a deep sleep.

The next day his mind was clearer.

"Doc," he croaked, "what's it all about? What's the matter with me? Why do I sing and laugh? I've always been a model prisoner before, Doc."

He tugged at the restraining jacket.

"Take these things off me so I can get up for awhile, will yuh please, Doc?" he pleaded. Then he lapsed into a singing spell.

He was in the same room with Joe Kalinoski, who was found butting his head against the wall of his concrete cell. Kalinoski, too, was in a restraining jacket – screaming and crying as his tortured mind devilled him. It was not a pretty picture. Kalinoski was in one bed, writhing and shrieking and Capone was in the other, bellowing gleefully in song, oblivious to Kalinoski. A screen was ordered and placed between the two beds. The officials were that considerate of Capone.

That evening, the restraining jacket was removed. It made no difference to him. He was happy either way.

On the fifth day of his collapse, two San Francisco psychiatrists came to the Island. They were there to discuss the transfer of June and Kalinoski to Springfield, the institution for the mentally ill. But they came, more so, to determine the extent of Capone's mental condition.

"Mr. Capone," he was asked, "do you remember singing songs in Italian the other night?"

"Sure, I was cheering the boys up."

"Weren't you singing at an unusual hour, when everybody was asleep?"

"Not to my knowledge, doctor. I don't remember what time it was when I was singing. I – I want you to do anything you can to help me. Anything at all. I will do whatever you want me to do to cure me."

"Tell me, Mr. Capone, have you noticed lately that you forget things more easily?"

"Well, Doc," he reflected, "do you want to know the truth? I noticed that for the past four months I have been forgetting things that I know I shouldn't forget. I can't seem to help myself."

One psychiatric report stated Capone should have treatment as soon as possible, otherwise he would be in an incurable state. Later, after he calmed down and ceased singing, Capone was placed in a private room. Although he was able to get around quite easily, other hospital prisoners brought his food to him. He rested from day to day and busied himself with writing letters and reading his many magazines.

"Say, Doc," he pleaded. "I want to get back to work, out in the yard. I'll get soft up here."

I told him he had better stay in the hospital and rest.

"I don't want to get out of shape," he mused. "I did a lot of exercise up here this morning – sitting-up exercises. That's one thing working in the yard has done for me – sheared off my weight."

In those mentally gloomy days that followed, he looked forward to the visits of his wife, Mae.

"It will be a swell day when she comes to see me at the end of this month," he sighed.

In the nightmare that is the Rock, the exiled Capone had one glimmer of reality, one bit of contact with the outside world – the regular visits of his wife. She and their son, who attended Notre Dame University, kept Capone's courage buoyed at Alcatraz. He was proud of his son's grades.

"He's a smart kid – plenty smart," he boasted.

Mae Capone stuck to her man, despite the underworld saying, "A wife won't stick to her man in prison more than a year." Theirs was a romance that endured since childhood. Mae Coughlin was sixteen when they were married. Capone was seventeen. They attended school together and were working in the same box factory when they eloped and pledged themselves to love, honor and obey .... Even the bleak walls of Alcatraz could not part them.

Her visits were shrouded in mystery. During the hectic days in Chicago, Capone shielded her from the notoriety that enmeshed him. He kept her cloistered in the background. She was seldom seen in public with him. Even during his income-tax evasion trial, she was never in court. Capone did not want her molested by prying reporters or photographers. Similarly, on her trips to and from her Florida home, Capone saw to it that reporters didn't annoy her.

As a result, her comings and goings were elusive and wraith-like, reminiscent of some mystery woman out of a spy yarn. She donned a blonde wig, then bought an airline or railroad ticket under an assumed name. On arrival in San Francisco, she persisted in cloaking her identity under a fictitious name. Sometimes she would stay at one of the swanky hotels, other times in an unobtrusive, side street hostelry.

She got around the rigid Alcatraz rule that decreed close relatives might visit a prisoner only one day a month. Mae saw her man two days in succession. She accomplished this by visiting Capone on the last day of the month, then returning to visit him the next day, the first day of the month. On the way from her hotel to catch the Alcatraz launch, she took several taxis, travelling a zigzag route to throw off any reporters who might be on her trail.

Mae didn't have much time to talk to Capone. They met in the visitor's room, under a guard's surveillance and talked through the diaphragm in the glass partition. They sat chatting back and forth. As with the other prisoners and the loved ones who visited them, there was no show of emotion, no parting kiss, no affectionate pat on the shoulder, with a tearful, "Be brave." The glass partition prevented that.

The government cooperated in keeping Mrs. Capone's visits secret and in seeing that she was not annoyed by reporters. Heavily armed military police and soldiers were on duty at the government dock where she boarded the Alcatraz boat and later disembarked. Let any photographer or reporter saunter onto the dock and they were promptly asked about their business. When the military police learned they were reporters, they were escorted off the long dock. Let them refuse and a hardwood club was raised menacingly.

Shortly after Capone's mental collapse, San Francisco reporters had a hunch she would be visiting him. Their intuition proved correct. They knew she was as elusive as a smoke ring and that they would not be allowed on the government dock. So the photographers climbed onto an adjoining pier some distance away and waited for her with telescopic lenses.

Cameras were trained on the gangplank of the government boat. A taxi pulled up to the craft – a woman in a mink coat climbed out and walked briskly up the gangplank. The cameras clicked. The photographers had their pictures. But they knew that the finished photographs would be fuzzy and indistinct – the distance was too great despite their telescopic lenses. Besides, they were ordered to get close-ups.

They waited for the boat to return. When they saw her walk down the gangplank and enter a waiting taxi, they sprinted to their cars and watched her cab leave the dock. They sped after her. Glancing back, Mae discovered she was being followed. She made a deal with her cab driver – there would be a greenback for him if he out distanced her pursuers.

The cab leaped ahead, streaked through stop signals, tore through one-way streets, zigzagged, careened dizzily around corners, and snaked in and out of traffic. The reporters were forced to give up the pursuit, losing the cab in the thick downtown traffic. But they weren't so easily vanquished. They made elaborate preparations for the following day, when she would make her second visit to Capone.

Six cars waited for her at the end of the dock. With them was a San Francisco motorcycle officer. The reporters wanted him along to see that no traffic laws were violated in this chase. The officer was instructed to flag down Mrs. Capone's cab should it go through a stop sign, travel the wrong way through a one-way street or exceed the speed limit.

They saw Mrs. Capone's cab drive up to the dock and watched her sail for Alcatraz. She returned several hours later and got into the waiting cab. The chase was on. The motorcycle officer sped up to the cab and cautioned the driver. The driver, in turn, wagged his head and said he would be careful. Mrs. Capone was hunched in the rear seat, the collar of her mink coat held high over her face. The chase took on the aspects of a funeral procession, the cars following one after the other and the cab driver maintaining a slow pace.

With the motorcycle officer riding alongside, the cab driver halted at each stop signal and waited patiently for mechanical intersection signals to flash from red to green. During these periodic pauses, the photographers piled out of their cars and, with equipment flying, sprang up to the cab, clustered around it, and clicked pictures of Mae Capone crouched in the rear. She ignored them, drawing her fur collar higher.

The cab sped through the San Francisco financial district, along the Embarcadero, then up the approach of the mighty San Francisco-Oakland Bridge. And in stately procession the reporters followed. At the point on the span where the San Francisco limits ended and Oakland began, the motorcycle officer left the parade – he no longer had jurisdiction – and the cab picked up speed.

The chase continued through Oakland, Hayward, and San Jose. When the cab speedometer ticked off seventy miles, the driver swung off the road for gas at a combination service station and lunchroom near the town of Morgan Hill. Persistent reporters climbed out of their cars to stretch their legs. Some ordered sandwiches. One reporter went up to Mae – still huddled in the rear of the cab – and addressed the teepee of mink that was shielding her.

"Mrs. Capone," he said, "we hate like hell to have to do this to you. We realize you must be pretty broken up, having just seen Al after his collapse and what with all us guys ready to chase you to hell and gone. So – well, to prove that we're not such wolves – could we bring you a cup of coffee, or a sandwich? You must be hungry and tired."

The mink teepee parted and two frightened eyes peeked out.

"What – what can I do so you'll go away and stop following me?" she asked.

"Well," said the reporter, "all we want is a picture. I think that's all the others want, too."

"Very well," replied Mae. "I'll let you take pictures. But I won't show all my face. Just half of it."

Yes, the reporters agreed, all they wanted was a picture. Any kind of picture, as long as it was a close-up. Besides, they were getting fed up with the chase. It was proving monotonous. Photographers surrounded the cab. Thrusting their cameras through the windows, they shot picture after picture of Mae Capone cowering in the rear seat clutching the mink coat collar with trembling, black-gloved hands.

Asked what Al was suffering from, she replied it was merely dejection, that his spirit was broken. However, the government's official report on his condition, released from Washington, contradicted her. Capone, the report said, was mentally ill; his condition was not brought about by his confinement in Alcatraz. It was due to something he suffered previous to his incarceration.

(My father told me many times that he treated Capone for syphilis.)

Prisoners got fresh air and a view of the new Golden Gate Bridge during their weekend recreation periods.

THE LONELIEST MAN ON ALCATRAZ

Since the first day he arrived at Alcatraz, the other prisoners shunned him, as though he were some loathsome thing.

In the mess hall, those sitting on either side of him inched away. When he asked other prisoners to pass the milk or sugar, they ignored him and continued eating.

During the recreation periods, he would amble up to a group of guffawing, joking prisoners and try to join them. Or, if they were short a man in some game that was starting, he volunteered to play. But they walked away and left him standing alone.

Amid the clatter of a prison workshop, he felt the eyes of his shop mates and, when looking up, saw their scowling faces. Marching back and forth to the mess hall or to the yard, he heard a whispered "Goddam baby snatcher" spat from the corner of someone's mouth.

At night, above the sloshing of the waves and the moaning of the foghorn, he heard hoarse contemptuous voices sneer,

"The gates of hell are closed to baby snatchers. Ynnnnnah!"

A guard overheard it, too, and bellowed, "Quiet."

Even the guards despised him. During a cold spell, when he asked for a blanket, one guard leered at him,

"So maybe you gave the little Weyerhaeuser kid a blanket when you snatched him, eh?"

Harmon Waley, baby snatcher, was the loneliest man on Alcatraz. He was as friendless and alone as though he was a castaway on some deserted tropical island. The stigma "baby snatcher" set him apart from the other prisoners. Ruthless killers, bank robbers and gang tycoons that they were, they refused to condone baby snatching.

"The dirty rat, picking on a little kid," they would scowl. "A kid can't fight back. Hell, he hadn't got the nerve to try and stick up a bank, or shoot it out with a cop. So he snatches a kid!"

Ignored, cursed and leered at, Waley seethed with indignation. While toiling over the mangle in the laundry, he ranted to the prisoner working beside him.

"All right, all right. Take it easy! All you have to do is feed it in. I've got to take it out. Slow down, damnit! I'm doing 40 years here. I've got plenty of time."

Capone – the prisoner working beside him – eyed him with disgust.

"You ----- kid snatcher," Cappone said softly.

Waley was furious. He grabbed a wad of soggy, moist laundry and flung it at Capone. It smacked against his face. Capone wiped the soapy water from his eyes and then tore into Waley, fists flying. He picked up a chair and started clouting Waley. Soon guards broke it up.

The prisoner's antagonism against Waley broke his spirit. He became listless, indifferent. Rebelling against the entire prison set-up, he bluntly announced he didn't care what happened to him, life was too miserable at Alcatraz.

First, he went on a hunger strike. For seventeen consecutive days he refused to eat.

On the seventeenth day, I visited Waley.

"How about eating, Waley?" I asked. "This isn't doing you any good. If you don't eat, we'll just have to give you the tube and pour it down."

Waley grimaced.

"I don't care. You can hose me with that tube day and night. The tube going into my nose and down my stomach doesn't bother me like it does other guys. I'm not eating."

I inserted the tube and poured down a pitcher of hot broth. Several times Waley paled and became nauseated and regurgitated. As the broth bubbled up, the guard holding the pitcher caught it and poured it down again, saying,

"As many times as it comes up, it will go down again."

"I don't give a goddam. You can give it to me with vomit puke, snot and all. What the hell do I care? I'm not eating until I get what I want. If it takes forty years, too. I'll tell you want I want. I want out of this goddam stinking joint."

"I want to go back to McNeil's – that's where I was sentenced. There was no damn reason to transfer me here. I'm tired of the agitation and persecution here and getting the glassy-eye."

"I'll tell you what else I want. I want some time off. There are guys in here with murder raps and they get out after ten years. I didn't murder anybody. My crime isn't as bad as that. All I did was kidnap a little kid!"

"Hell, I have to do fifteen years before I have a chance for a possible parole."

Waley remained adamant and kept his vow not to eat. We continually resorted to tube feeding. Following one feeding of cream of tomato soup, Waley belched.

"Pretty good soup," he grinned. "Doesn't taste bad. It's too bad I'm all worked up, otherwise I might be eating and enjoying it."

"There's a good dinner waiting for you Thanksgiving Day if you start eating."

"Nuts. I left all my good dinners behind when I came to this hell hole."

After another tube feeding, the guard removed the tube from Waley's nose and wiped it with a towel. Waley leaned back and snickered.

"I say, old bean," he said in a silly-ass English impersonation, "that was deucedly swell service. Now how about a finger bowl, my good man?"

In the midst of his hunger strike, Waley announced he would not budge from his bed. He made that clear to the guards when they approached him prior to another tube feeding.

"I'm not getting out of bed. Carry me if you want. If you want me to shave, then you shave me. If you want me to take a bath, then you carry me down and bathe me. I'm not doing a damn thing by myself any more. Get it?"

"Get out of bed," a guard commanded. "Get out or we'll drag you out!"

"Not on your life. Not while there's so goddam much antagonism against me."

"You're asking for it, Waley – GET UP!" the guard thundered.

Whereupon Waley was forcibly hauled out of bed, slammed down on the floor and tube fed. That afternoon, he walked voluntarily into the hospital.

"What's the trouble now, Waley?" I asked.

"Oh," Waley grinned, "I – ah – bumped myself against the wall and hurt my hand and forehead."

"Kind of peculiar, bumping yourself, isn't it?"

"Yeahhhhhh."

His left ring finger was puffed and swollen. The letters M-E-T-Z were tattooed on his fingers.

"That's my middle name – Metz," he explained.

The following day he was once again hauled out of bed and tube fed. That night, when I visited him, I found the cell a shambles. Waley yanked the blankets and mattress off the bed, piling them teepee-fashion in a corner. His clothes were strewn about and he flooded the cell by letting the washbasin run over. He was lying nude and shivering on the cement floor, the water swirling around him.

"What's the idea, Waley?"

"Just getting sick. That's all. I want to get out of here. What's the difference if they take me out one way or another – feet first, in a box, is as good a way as any."

I ordered him to get off the floor.

"If I get sick, they'll send me to the hospital," he continued. "That seems to be the only damn place around here where prisoners are left alone."

The cell adjoining his was stripped of everything in it, including the bed and the chains from which the bed was suspended from the wall. Waley was placed in this cell. He plopped himself on the cold floor and announced he would hang himself with the blankets left him. So the blankets were removed.

The warden was notified.

"Admit him to the hospital where he can be watched," the warden ordered.

Waley was brought to the hospital and placed in a restraining jacket, remaining flat on his back and motionless during the night. The next morning he went to isolation again because he was neither sick nor insane. He was a discipline problem.

Guards "shook down" the cell from top to bottom, assuring themselves he concealed nothing with which he might harm himself. The cell was judged free of any hidden objects. Waley was led into it entirely nude except for a pair of shoes from which the laces were extracted. Laces were potential nooses – great for strangulation.

Less than twenty minutes later, a passing guard saw Waley hacking at himself with a broken safety razor blade. He was bleeding from his arms and wrists and had smeared blood over his face. This gave him an eerie slaughterhouse look. The guard was aghast.

"Stop that, Waley!" he shouted.

The guard hauled him out and brought him to the hospital.

"Tough luck, you passing by," Waley lamented.

"You fool," the guard glared, "do you want to kill yourself?"

"What do you think?"

Despite the smeared blood, his condition was not serious. He was bleeding only slightly from small lacerations of the right wrist and at the bends of both elbows. Smearing blood over his face was a gesture to make it appear more serious and terrifying.

"Where did you have the razor blade hidden?" I asked him.

"What's the difference – I had it a long time."

His belongings were searched. It was discovered he had concealed the blade in the sole of his shoe.

"You didn't really want to kill yourself, did you?" I wanted to know.

Waley shrugged his shoulders.

"I don't know, doc. Maybe I lost my nerve. Maybe I just wanted to get into the hospital. What does it matter what I do, here at Alcatraz?"

He was informed he would remain in the hospital, in restraint, until his wounds healed. Then it was back to isolation.

"All right," he scowled, "let them send me back. When I go down to isolation again I still won't want anything that belongs to this place – I don't want their goddam food or their blankets or their clothes. You'll just have to keep feeding me with that goddam tube. I won't eat until I'm on a train leaving here."

The other men in isolation believed Waley was blowing his top.

"Serves the damn baby snatcher right," they grunted. "Just another nut, eh? Well, that's what'll happen to us, too, if they don't give us some books to read. We'll all string ourselves up if we don't get some light bulbs and magazines soon."

Despite the days of tube feeding, inactivity and restraint, Waley weakened very little. He was young and strong and stubborn. At times he grew philosophical and discussed the kidnapping.

"I don't know how I got into that mess," he said to me one night after a knockdown and drag-out tube-feeding bout. "I got all tangled up in it and couldn't get out. I was in jail before and ran across a pal I met there. That was in Salt Lake. I went east to look for a job, couldn't find anything, and came back to Salt Lake. I met up with Mahan, my former cellmate."

"Well, I went around with him while he looked over a few layouts to pull a few jobs, but I never pulled anything with him. Then one day he read in the newspaper where the old man Weyerhaeuser, the little kid's grandfather, died. It gave him an idea. He put down the paper and said it would bring a lot of dough if we snatched the kid for ransom."

"I told him he was crazy, that he couldn't get away with it, and that I wouldn't have a thing to do with it. But I went along with him while he got the layout and figured out how he would pull the job."

"We prowled around the kid's school. When the kid got out he didn't wait for his chauffeur but walked along the tennis court near the school and came by our car. Before I knew it, Mahan grabbed the kid, pulled him into the car and sped off. From then on, I was in it – whether I liked it or not. And so here I am. My wife even got twenty years. She was innocent and didn't know a damn thing about it. But she got the time, anyhow. Now she's at the pen in Michigan. She's stopped writing to me. I don't blame her."

Other times he cursed Alcatraz in macabre soliloquies.

"Listen to the foghorn. The Alcatraz Symphony. Beautiful, eh? Goddam noise drives you screwy. You've gotta get used to it. Too bad if it gets the best of you. Makes you want to jump out of your skin. Listen to the cellhouse doors. You're in a concrete cell, two feet across and five feet back. Clanging noise of the doors ringing in your head. It's all right when the doors open for you to get out. You get away from it for a while. Go to the mess hall to eat. To the yard to play a little. To work. Yeah, that's all right."

"But how about the end of the day when you drag yourself back to the cell. The doors clang and you're locked in. The noise makes your head swim. And then the damn silence of the cellhouse. No talking. Like a tomb. God, that's worse than the noise, sometimes. It makes your head reel. Feels like your brains are busting out of your scalp. Your world is a black pit, two feet across and five feet back. You want to get out, but can't. Two feet across and five feet back. You want to run and gulp in air and see endless stretches of land before you. But you can't because you're in a grave two feet across and five feet back. You want to scream and bang things around. But you don't. Because you would go to the dungeon if you raised hell. Sure. Spend nineteen days in a smaller, darker hole. A meal every fourth day. Bread and water. Sleep on a cold cement floor. One blanket. All you can do is think, think, think. If you could only stop thinking, but you can't."

"You think of sunshine and trees and women and think how swell it was to be free. But you're not free, and there's no sunshine. It's just dark."

"The monotony is broken when the guard comes to see if you haven't committed suicide."

"He opens the door and a little light comes in, jabs into your eyes. A little fresh air comes in. It makes you suddenly realize the "hole" is foul and stinks. Then the door bangs closed and it's black and stifling again. It takes a little while before your eyes get accustomed to it again."

"Then you imagine you're seeing things in the dark. Those spook stories of how these dungeons used to hold Spanish prisoners flash before you. You imagine you hear chains rattling, and hear screams from some poor guy who's on the rack, in some nearby torture chamber."

"Then you come to with a start. You realize that you're alone. Maybe you think of your kid days. Gee, I used to be a funny kid. Had a lot of fun. And then later I got into trouble. Maybe if I were a little smarter I could have gotten away with it. Sure, I made some mistakes. I can see them now."

"Then you think of death. You figure maybe you can kill yourself, and get away from it all. You wonder how it would feel to dangle from the top of your cell with a noose made from strips of blanket around your neck, choking you, cutting off the air, making your tongue stick out, until you see fiery cartwheels in front of your eyes, then unconsciousness."

"Or you wonder how would it be with a razor blade. Strangulation's too slow, too painful. What happens when you bleed to death? What happens when you die? Where do you go? Is there any pain? Do you feel anything? Do you just end up stiff, hard and lifeless? Something that turns rotten and decays away?"

"Then you figure maybe a bullet would be sweet. You could get it by climbing over the fence like poor old Joe Bowers did. You can get a bullet in your back if you attack somebody. But who? The warden? The deputy? No, they're pretty good guys."

"Why not that guard who's got it in for you? All the cons hate him. Sure, so you plan it all out. In the mess hall? No. The yard! That's it – the yard. You pass within ten feet of him there. Get a shiv from one of the shops. How many steps will you have to take? Time it just right. The guard in the tower will be ready. Jab the shiv into the blue coat. See the blood spurt out. See the amazed look on his mug as he falls. Then wait for the tower guards' bullets to come plowing into you."

"So they bump you off. No more silence. No more clanging bells. No more wind howling through your cell. No more surf bombarding the Island. No more getting up in the morning. No more work. No more being herded around like a sheep. No more cons around here giving you the cold and glassy because you're a kid snatcher. But can you make yourself shove the shiv into a guard? You know damn well you can't because you're too yellow. You're afraid to die. You'd rather walk around here, a living corpse, breathing and eating, than be a dead one, planted for good."

The prison officials became concerned over Waley's hunger strike and listless attitude. The deputy warden visited him at the hospital, eyed him silently for awhile, then shook his head and said,

"Still acting like a Hoosier, eh?"

(Hoosier was a prison slang word meaning naïve.)

"Sure, I'm still acting like a Hoosier," Waley retorted. "And I'm going to keep on acting that way."

"You're hurting nobody but yourself, Waley."

"I know it. I've got it all figured out. I'm gonna keep it up. You can keep your goddam food and blankets and tube feed me all you want. I'm not compromising."

The deputy stared at Waley solemnly.

"I didn't come up here to compromise with you. Who the hell do you think you are? We won't promise you a damn thing. You can stay right here, tied down in a restraining jacket for the next hundred years. I don't give a damn."

Waley tsk-tsk-tsked.

"Keep your shirt on, deputy. I'm doing this rap. If I prefer to serve my time this way, all right. It's me who will suffer. If I die, just bury me."

The deputy glared with disgust, muttering, "You can't argue with a Hoosier," and stomped away. Out of Waley's earshot, he explained,

"I tried to get him mad, doctor. Sometimes you can get them to cut out their foolishness that way."

Meanwhile, Waley was chuckling in bed.

"Wow, I sure got him mad, didn't I? He looked like he was going to burst a blood vessel. Well, they can break me in everything except my will and spirit. They can't break that – not in a million years."

So the nasal feeding continued. And Waley was restrained day and night. Occasionally he asked, "How am I doing, doc?" I said he certainly wasn't losing weight on the tube-fed eggnog. But he was growing weaker from lack of exercise. He was eventually taken out of restraint and compelled to walk up and down the hospital for twenty minutes daily.

"Christ, I'm dizzy," he gasped the first day of his enforced exercise, staggering across the room.

"You'll be steady in a few minutes," I told him.

"To hell with this stuff – it hurts – it's making me sick. I want to get back to bed."

"No you don't. Keep walking. The exercise will do you good."

Groping his way along by supporting himself on the other beds, Waley walked back and forth. Soon he was able to maneuver without support.

"I'm dying for a smoke," he said.

A sack of tobacco and cigarette paper was given to him. With a slow jerking motion, Waley rolled himself a cigarette – his first in days. He smoked incessantly the full twenty minutes of his exercise period.

"All right, Waley," I said when the time was up, "we're going to have another little tying up party again. Let's go."

A sickly smile illuminated Waley's face.

"And I'm it," he laughed weakly. "That walk was pretty good."

After nine days and nights of being bound in bed with a restraining jacket, and after 26 days of tube feeding, Waley made a startling announcement – he was willing to eat again. The diet of broth and eggnog and soup, administered through the tube, was too much for him. He acknowledged defeat and was removed from the ward and placed in a cell by himself in the hospital.

Three days later he removed the light bulb from the ceiling of his cell and hid it, evidently planning to hurt himself with the glass. The bulb was noticed missing and a shakedown followed. It was later found. Now Waley's bed was removed. He was left with only the mattress on the floor.

Later that day, I inquired as to his health. This provoked a hysterical outburst punctuated by sobs and oaths. He launched into a diatribe against Alcatraz and justice. Pacing to and fro, gesturing and bellowing, he fumed,

"I'm sick of this agitation against me here. I haven't any friends. They call me a kid snatcher. The cons don't like me and the officials don't like me. What kind of a goddam place is this, anyhow? My nerves can't stand much more of this. They're raw and frazzled to beat hell now."

"I treated that Weyerhaeuser kid fine. I gave him ice cream and candy and everything. I must have treated him good. He didn't even want to go home!"

Tears welled in his eyes as he continued to storm and rage.

"They don't give me my letters. My mother's sick. She's only got a few more years to live. That's why I hate this place. When I was at McNeil's Island, I could see her. Then they transferred me here. She can't afford to come all the way out here. I'll never see her again!"

He cursed the prison officials.

"They won't let me learn anything! I want to learn how to play a saxophone, so that when my time's ready for parole I can show the parole board I'm capable of getting a job as a musician. I have to learn something to show the parole board! I haven't any other trade or profession except machine gunner."

"Oh, so you didn't know I was one, eh? I was a soldier of fortune in Mexico – something equivalent to a top sergeant. If I could get the hell out of here, I'd beat it to China and fight for them. In Mexico, I got about two hundred bucks a month. I like to fight, damn it! If I die in battle, I know goddam well where I'm going – to Valhalla, where all fighting men go. There's plenty of wine and feasting and women, too."

Waley knew it was useless to go on another hunger strike. So he decided to feign insanity, hoping to be transferred to Springfield as a mental patient.

"There's a man hanging outside my window on a rope!" he screamed one night. "He comes in and stands in front of me all the time. Somebody else comes out of the drain pipe in the washbasin and makes faces at me, too."

He tired of making believe he was insane and was brought out of isolation and into the hospital again. For a while, he was content to remain quiet, busying himself reading music magazines.

"A hell of a way to have to learn music," he grumbled. "From magazines. Imagine! But there's some good stuff in here for physicians, too, doctor. It tells about diseases musicians get from blowing instruments."

He delighted in agitating the mentally ill patients being held for observation. He coaxed them to create disturbances, told them to swash their bedpans against the bars and yammer. The unfortunate mentally ill patients delighted in cavorting and making disturbances for Waley.

In the midst of one of Waley's coaxed-up outbursts, a critically ill prisoner was brought to the hospital. It was Fred Brown, who had but eight more months to serve for conspiracy in a post office robbery. Brown's condition grew worse. Blood transfusions were needed. The prisoners were informed of his condition, blood donors were asked to volunteer. Most of them were sympathetic.

"Of course I'll volunteer," Capone said. "Any time."

"Sure," said Kelly. "I don't particularly like the fellow, but it's okay with me. I'd even give blood to help a dying animal."

Another prisoner wrote a note to me in which he volunteered. The note, written on blue-ruled notebook paper started out,

"Re transfusion," and continued, "I was given shots for syphilis in Iowa State Prison in 1932. After giving me a few they learned they had erred by a mistake in labels on the blood tests. So another test of myself was negative. I've had five tests since – just to be sure. All were negative. If my blood is the correct type, I will be pleased to give the fellow a quart. I have plenty. No fooling."

Despite the dying prisoner's condition, Waley persisted in raising periodic rumpuses in the hospital, yelling and cursing and smashing his bedpan against the bars of his cell. The other hospital patients were furious at Waley's actions.

"Can you imagine the damned baby snatcher raising hell while a man's dying," they swore. "We ought to kill the bastard. He's got no respect for nothing."

When Waley was informed that Brown had died, he showed no emotion. Later he asked for paper and pencil and cloistered himself in his cell. Several hours later, he handed me a poem.

"Ah – er," he began, "here's a poem I wrote for Brown. Maybe I was a heel cutting up while – ah – he was here. Maybe the – ah – other boys would like to see it. I've called it *Sands*. Maybe it could be a sort of obituary for the poor guy, huh?"

Sands
by Harmon Waley

Like shifting, gleaming grains of sand
This life runs on toward the end.
As sunsets gently-tinted rays,
To hilltops softened shadows land.

And as the grains go sifting by,
Seem lead by fairy hand unseen,
So life goes on with changing tread
From dark to light and fat to lean.

We learn, and yet we nothing know,
Of life, or sand, nor where they go
When reaching yon black abyss pit
Where swiftly falling they expend
Into the nothingness of it.

Then two new mentally ill prisoners were brought to the hospital and placed in adjoining cells to Waley. One was Joe Kalinoski, who persisted in thumping his head against the cell wall. The other was Harold June, who climbed gorilla-like to the top of his cell and raved and ranted. At first Waley joined in the fun. But soon their incessant ravings, incoherent sentences, and mumbling got on his nerves. He stood it as long as he could.

One day he said,

"I'm licked. I'll go back to work. If I stay next to those guys any longer I'll end up making faces, too."

And so Harmon Waley went back to the work-a-day routine. The prisoners still ignored him, still whispered "baby snatcher!" But Waley resigned himself to his fate. No longer did he make overtures to them.

"The only overtures I'm making are through my saxophone," announced the loneliest man on Alcatraz. "I'm gonna be the best goddam sax player in the country by the time my parole's ready."

Listening to the Alcatraz Symphony moan on the frequent foggy nights drove the prisoner's berserk.

Robinson

Virtually all his life – by his own admission – Thomas Robinson, Jr. groped for something. Contentment. Security. A regulated, orderly life. He cracked trying to fit himself into the social scheme of things. Then came the kidnapping of Mrs. Alice Stoll in Louisville, Kentucky and his sentence of life imprisonment.

Robinson was perhaps the most contented man on the Rock. The stringent rules enabled him to lead an orderly life for the first time in his 31 years. Prison bells told him when to get up, when to eat, and when to go to bed. Prison walls kept him from the temptations he was unable to forgo on the outside – women, money, jewels, and good times.

Outside he never held a job longer than a few months due to "emotional instability," as diagnosed by the prison officials. At Alcatraz, he resigned himself to his work in the prison tailor shop. He performed expertly because he no longer strived to fit himself into the scheme of things.

This is his own story, the document of a man who found himself, as he told it to me.

"I was born in Nashville, Tennessee, the only child of a family well above the average in wealth, education, background, social and business success. My mother was an accomplished musician on the piano and organ. My father possessed a Bachelor of Law degree as well as one in civil engineering. He was a thirty-second degree Mason and a Shriner. He was associated for nearly 30 years with the

Nashville Bridge Company, most of the time as a high-salaried general manager.

He was at one time the leading steel construction engineer in the south and a politician of some influence.

I grew up as a normal child until I reached the last of my grammar school days. I went to Sunday school and church, and later the young men's bible class, of which my father was the leader. Father was also church Deacon. I joined the Boy Scouts, worked up to a First Class Scout, and lacked only a few merit badges to make me an Eagle Scout, the highest class in the organization. Father was scoutmaster of our troop.

In school I made top grades, took piano lessons after school, and played in several small recitals. I also went in for all kinds of athletics. In short, I enjoyed all the advantages of a perfect home and community life. Then came my first bad break. I became very ill while I was in the eighth grade. First, I had an attack of malaria, then influenza. This developed into double pneumonia and pleurisy. It ended in tuberculosis. My family sent me to a sanitarium. I was cured there but developed a terrible inferiority complex, suffering all those illnesses, a complex for which I blamed many of my subsequent misfortunes.

I couldn't go in for athletics anymore the way I used to. My family engaged a tutor to make up my losses in schoolwork. Then they sent me to Wallace Preparatory School, an exclusive private school for boys. Because I couldn't indulge in sports anymore, I devoted all my time to study. In my senior year, I took the prize for the highest mark in Latin. Mother bought me a car of my own and I made plenty of friends.

I matriculated to Vanderbilt University in 1926 and enrolled in the law school. I made the Pi Kappa Alpha social fraternity and the Gamma Eta Gamma legal fraternity. In all my two and one-half years at college, I did well in my studies, received leading marks in many of my subjects. I was dating girls in the debutante and Junior League groups and was practically engaged to one of these girls at the time.

Then fate dealt me another bum card. I had been having relations with a girl on the 'other side of the tracks.' I was served with a warrant, charging me with the violation of the age of consent law. I had to marry her to keep out of jail, but we agreed to get a divorce later. A few weeks after this marriage, the girl bore a nine-pound, full term baby.

As I had known this girl for only seven months before the baby came, I sued for an annulment and it was granted. I also asked that the child be illegitimatized because the girl and her family were becoming very demanding of money. The court granted this also. To show you how I was framed, the girl, during the court trial, admitted intercourse with several other men at the time the child was conceived, and was forced to declare she did not know me at the time. A letter was produced in which she accused another boy of being the father of the child.

The whole affair caused a scandal. It resulted in being ostracized from my fine friends. Everybody cut me dead. The girl I was in love with broke our engagement. A fellow has to have friends and I started finding them among boys and girls who were not exactly what you'd call socially prominent. I guess I developed a psychosis, worrying over the whole mess. My inferiority complex increased, though I continued my law studies. Had I not gotten myself into that scandal I would have been taken into a prominent law firm after I graduated. But that prospect was scotched now.

I had a good job offered me by the Briggs Body Works of Detroit, and I decided to drop my law studies and accept it. Sometime afterwards I married a girl I met while I was in college. I soon found out the marriage was a mistake but by that time I didn't care much anymore. All ambition had died in me. I don't think my mind was normal at the time. Six months later I lost my job. That was in March 1929.

Then I had my first run-in with the law. I had to have money and I wasn't working. I filled out two search warrants and entered two homes, posing as a deputy sheriff. I took jewelry valued from $11,000 to $44,000. I did not use a gun or any sort of violence.

Three months later they caught me. I returned all of the jewelry and my father paid for its recovery. I was indicted for robbery but my attorneys got me off on an insanity plea and I was committed to a Tennessee hospital for the insane. There I stayed for 11 months. Then the criminal charges against me were "nolle prossed" by the state and my father was appointed my legal guardian.

I was transferred to another hospital for the insane as a private pay patient. After three months, my father took me out after putting up a $500 bond as security for my behavior, a bond that he renewed each year. However, I was not released from the hospital as cured and at no time have I been declared legally sane. That's why I didn't think I should be held responsible for any criminal acts I committed thereafter. The judicial decree of insanity and of dementia praecox was still in force against me.

After I left the insane hospital, my wife and I went to live with my parents. A son was born to us while I was locked up and my problem now was to get a job. My father was still politically powerful and had plenty of business connections. None of that seemed to help me now. Nobody wanted to employ a man with an insanity record.

I wrote letters of application to every friend and possible employer I could think of. I suffered nothing but disappointments. I'm telling you this to show you that I wanted to work, not to be a criminal. I had good character references from previous employers. I held more than a dozen short-term jobs since I was 15, working during vacations for pocket money. Several times I had worked for my father's bridge company.

But all of my efforts to obtain employment commensurate with my education and business training failed now. In the end, I had to take humble jobs for which I was unfit – janitor, filling station attendant, timekeeper and field laborer. It's hard for me to put into words my gloom and despair as I went across the country, taking some labor job, saving money when I could, so that I might go to a distant town where I was not known. Then the torture of going through the whole weary business of answering want ads, visiting employment offices, slaving half the night over a typewriter, and writing letters of application. So many times there were jobs that seemed to be just within my reach when something mysterious happened and they fell through. Then a prospective employer told me that one of the men I had been giving as a reference was blabbing about the old robbery charge. I grew more careful about the references I gave out, checking and re-checking each one. But always a breath of the past rose to prevent me from getting a real job. I found out that employers might sometimes be willing to hire an ex-prisoner but not a former prisoner of an insane asylum.

To add to my miseries, my father's bridge company failed during this period and threw him out of work. After a lifetime in steel he could not readily turn his hand to anything else. My mother lost her $20,000 home.

In 1933, I got a break and obtained a job as payroll timekeeper under bond for the Dupont Company. Eight months later, my luck crashed again. I was falsely accused of stealing $8 from a girl, while her girlfriend said I had taken two rings from her. The girl told police I took the rings from her while we were driving on a Tuesday afternoon.

Unknown to her, I was working on a job 16 miles away that afternoon and I was able to bring my boss with the records to prove it. The charges were dismissed and the girl was severely rebuked. This incident brought my past record to light and I was discharged from the company.

I landed in Chicago with $6 and took a janitor's job at $22 a week. I was fired four months later for inefficiency. By this time, my life was approaching a climax. I had become so bitter over my bad luck and so nervous I couldn't hold any kind of job. I was beset with complexes and wild ideas. I guess that was what made me pull the job that landed me on Alcatraz.

All my hatred and resentment centered on one of my former employers, a man named C. C. Stoll. I had always given him as a reference when I applied for work and by now I was pretty sure it was he who had given me a black name wherever I went.

In the fall of 1934, I began to plan revenge on that guy. I guess my mind was a little unbalanced. My wife and I were living in an apartment in Indianapolis. I sent her home to her mother so she would be out of the way. Then I set to work preparing a ransom note. You could see I wasn't an experienced criminal by the kind of note I wrote. I didn't realize I would get my father into trouble when I named him as intermediary for the $50,000 ransom money. I even gave my own address. I must have been nuts!

With this crazy ransom note I drove to Louisville and called at the home of Mrs. Stoll, daughter-in-law of the man I planned to kidnap. I had known Mrs. Stoll when I was working for her father-in-law.

I asked her for money. She offered me some but it wasn't enough. I got mad. I told her if she didn't get more money, I would kidnap her husband instead of her father-in-law. We argued a lot. According to the subsequent testimony of the maid, we were in the apartment about three hours. Mrs. Stoll offered to go with me herself if I would leave her husband alone. We argued some more and she reached for a gun under her pillow. I hit her with a black jack but I didn't even knock her down. I then crossed out Mr. Stoll's name on the ransom note and wrote Mrs. Alice Speed Stoll's name. She put on a coat and we went out to my car.

She went voluntarily. On our way to my apartment in Indianapolis, we drove over a toll bridge guarded by police. I paid the toll in their presence. Mrs. Stoll certainly had a chance to call for help then, but she didn't.

Mrs. Stoll and I stayed in my apartment six days. I frequently went out to make phone calls and to mail letters. Many times Mrs. Stoll was left free to come and go. She did the cooking and stayed of her own accord. By this time, my wife was in on the kidnapping. She agreed to bring me the ransom money after my father received it, which he was forced to do. All this time, I never dreamed this would get my family or me into any legal entanglement.

To me this was a personal feud, a desire to get even with the Stolls. I never thought they would go to the police with it. I guess that shows how insane I was. I even felt I was doing my father a favor by making him intermediary.

My wife brought the $50,000 ransom money to me. Then she and Mrs. Stoll sat in my apartment for several hours while I made my getaway. I rode into Grand Central Station, New York with my picture in every paper.

For twenty months, I was a fugitive, though I stayed at the best hotels – the Hotel New Yorker, the Lexington, and the Waldorf Astoria. I bought a large wardrobe with the ransom money and went everywhere without arousing suspicion.

Then I met Jean Breese in a Greenwich Village nightclub. She was the woman who later put the finger on me. We met New Year's Eve in 1934 and began living together. We continued so for 16 months. I thought Jean was on the up and up. Several times I tested her but she always came through true blue.

Somebody recognized me in New York so Jean and I hopped a plane for Los Angeles. We rented a fine house in Santa Monica, bought a $3,200 sedan. We had memberships in several exclusive clubs and everything was going fine. Then I heard that my father and my wife were on trial for their part in the absurd kidnapping. I felt I had to help them, to get money to them.

So Jean and I drove to New York. Along the way we exchanged most of the ransom money for other bills. I succeeded in getting a sum of money to my family. My father and my wife were acquitted, I'm thankful to say. I was grateful to Jean and put aside a good slice of the ransom money for her, in care of her sister.

Jean and I decided the best place for me to hide would be the great open spaces. We agreed to buy a ranch and started out for New Mexico. I took an option on a ranch near Silver City. It was lonely out there, however, and soon we headed for southern California again. I had a notion to buy a ranch in the vicinity of Los Angeles or else in Nevada and breed dogs but we found that buying a ranch without telling who you were wasn't so easy.

In May 1936, when we were living in California, Jean got sore at me. Or maybe she just got tired. Anyway, she went to the G-men and told them where I was living. They came for me all right and flew me by special plane to Louisville. I sent for an attorney but he never showed up, though I paid him a large retainer. My mother and father came, however.

My mother pleaded with the judge to spare my life. Helpless, without legal counsel, I pleaded guilty and got a life sentence. They did not tell me I could change my plea of guilty within ten days. I am sure that with the right attorney I could have gotten off on an insanity plea. I was taken to Leavenworth.

All this time I had not the faintest idea that it was Jean who had turned me in. I refused to tell the G-men anything that might involve her. She visited me at Leavenworth and told me she was going to retain the best lawyers to get me out.

They gave me a mental test at Leavenworth and when a lot of questions answerable by 'right' or 'wrong' were put to me, I purposely tried to miss many of them. I thought if I got a low grade it would help my case. I understand I got one of the highest grades anyway.

I gave Jean my signature, which enabled her to get a box containing $7,500 of the ransom money from a Los Angeles storehouse. Sure, she got me two lawyers, but they only pretended to help me. They tricked me. Then Jean turned around and sold the story of the kidnapping to the Scripps-Howard Newspapers for $10,000, admitting in the story that it was she who turned me in.

When I found out, I saw red. I told the FBI that I would tell all. J. Edgar Hoover sent an agent to Leavenworth. For ten days and nights I typed the story of my life – 70,000 words of it. I told them I would go to court and testify against Jean. I thought this should make me deserving of clemency. But now I'm on Alcatraz and no action has been taken on my statement."

The government charged that Robinson bruised and beat Mrs. Stoll while he held her prisoner for six days. They also charged that he shot his wife during a brawl. This occurred when he found out that his wife wasn't going to business school as she told him. He grew suspicious. The gun was dropped during the altercation and Mrs. Robinson was shot in the leg.

Asked whether he ever handled firearms, Robinson replied,

"I am an expert rifle and pistol shot because of my years of hunting. But I have never participated in any armed robbery or things like that. In fact, I never saw any gangsters until I came to Alcatraz."

Federal authorities had letters from Jean Breese declaring that she turned Robinson in for his own good and because she loved him. She wrote that she would wait for him until he was released and once sent him a $10 money order, stating that his own mother could not afford to send him any money.

During the twenty months that G-men hunted Robinson, he was repeatedly reported to be masquerading as a woman. Robinson maintains it was this masquerade that enabled him to elude authorities for so long.

"I never dressed up as a woman," he said. "Once when I was driving with my wife she put her hat on me and painted up my face like a woman's. An officer stopped us and I received a $10 fine for disorderly conduct. Later, the detectives remembered that incident and thought I would be hiding out as a woman."

He told one amusing incident of his fugitive days. It happened in Silver City, where he paid a $300 deposit on an $8,500 ranch when he and Jean decided to settle down to a rustic life.

"We were having a drink in the Elks Club there," he related, "when somebody pointed out the local sheriff. I was told he was the man who caught Dillinger. My picture was posted everywhere so I was afraid he would recognize me. To make matters worse, Jean playfully took his 10-gallon hat and put it on my head to see how I would look. I turned red but still the sheriff didn't recognize me."

"After that I decided Silver City was hot and left town without getting back my deposit on the ranch."

When Robinson first arrived at Alcatraz, he worked in the kitchen. He liked that because he got the pick of the food, could have a daily shower and an hour in the yard. But he smashed his toe when a large iron kettle fell on it. He was taken to the prison hospital. While he was there, a hospital orderly became ill and quit his job. Robinson took it. He was enthusiastic at first but soon found that it was mostly floor polishing work rather than brainwork.

He asked for another job and was transferred to the prison tailor shop where he was content. Although he thought the law should overlook his past crimes because of the streak of insanity, he bore the law no special grudge. Authorities said he was fully adjusted to his surroundings, unlike the majority of prisoners. He spent his spare time reading and taking an active interest in current events.

Gulls inhabited Alcatraz Island and provided fodder for some.

His ancestors were solemn chieftains who once held court over tribal fires in ornate teepees. Now Thomas W. Wareagle squatted beside the Alcatraz incinerator, feeding garbage into its fiery maw. Wareagle was a full-blooded, teepee-born American Indian. Had he lived during the wars of the West, he would have been a fierce warrior, leading braves to battle the white invaders.

A lurid career of shootings, killings, bootlegging, violating the Mann Act, drinking, and peddling dope culminated in the kidnapping of a man in Tennessee. This made him eligible for Alcatraz. Wareagle chafed at the narrow confines on the Rock. He chafed even more over the lack of solitude his Indian nature demanded.

"Too many people here," he grumbled. "Too much noise. Too much doing. Wareagle like to go alone into woods, be alone with birds and deer." So Alcatraz authorities gave him the job of burning rubbish out on the cliffs, a task he liked because he could be alone for a stretch. The prisoners said he reverted to his woodland heritage there by luring gulls with bait from the dumps, snaring them and roasting them in the incinerator.

"Seagulls plenty tough," he grunted, "but better than pork and beans. I feed them garbage, pick the fattest ones, and wring their necks. Then I cover 'em with mud, roast 'em, and eat 'em. Wish I could get garlic to take wild fish taste out. Taste better, then."

Prison records show Wareagle was mentally deficient, due to a bullet wound in his head. He received it from an Alabama cattle rancher in a dispute over a fence more than twenty years hence.

G-men once cursed Wareagle's muddle-headed delusions. It was while they were hunting Frank Nash, the bank murderer who was later mowed down in the Kansas City railroad depot massacre.

Nash had just shot his way out of Leavenworth prison, wounding the warden. Wareagle was doing two years for violating the Mann Act and would be released shortly. He whispered to authorities that he knew Nash's hideout.

"Nash going back to Oklahoma," he told them, nodding sagely.

Harassed G-men, reluctant to overlook any tip, sprinted to Oklahoma. A little later, after he was released, Wareagle gave them another "tip."

"Wareagle see Nash," he said. "Wareagle make date with Nash to buy morphine. You come with Wareagle. Wareagle show you."

The government agents let Wareagle have a car. They followed him in another car. He led them through the woods and canyons of the Osage Hills. This went on for hours. At last, the exasperated G-men stopped Wareagle.

"Say, where IS this house where you were supposed to meet Nash?" they demanded.

Wareagle cringed. "Don't know, Boss," he whimpered. "I forgot."

"Come on, fellow, you don't just forget things like that. You show us that house or ELSE," the G-men threatened. Wareagle gulped. "All right, I try again," he muttered. Their wandering continued for a few more hours. At last, he drew up in front of an isolated house in a canyon.

"That the place. Nash – he in there. See, Wareagle show 'em."

With primed guns, the agents approached the house.

"Come out, Nash. We know you're in there," they shouted. A bewildered man appeared on the stoop. He was not Nash, nor was there any trace of the desperado in the house. It was just one of Wareagle's numerous delusions.

He had many of them on the Rock, like hearing voices that spoke to him in his cell – voices, he said, of his family and of dead spirits.

Psychiatrists attributed Wareagle's crime career to his quick temper and a self-vindication complex due to the vicissitudes of his none-too-happy childhood. His father, chief of the Osage Indian Tribe, was shot to death on the Indian Reservation in Oklahoma when he was five. His mother died when he was two. Then Chief Simon Loeho adopted him. Chief Loeho treated the orphan harshly but pampered his own children. Wareagle said he noticed this and felt woefully out of place. More and more, he went into the woods, preferring its rich solitude to the company of other children.

When he was nine, his foster father forced him to work in the fields from sun up to sun down. Once, said Wareagle, when he asked Chief Loeho if he could get a drink of water, the Chief whaled him across the head with a sassafras root. When Wareagle was 12, his foster father sent him out in the midst of a fierce thunderstorm to gather apples in the orchard. The boy made up his mind then to leave his people and seek a better life.

His opportunity came when a government agent took an interest in him and sent him to school at Blackwell, Oklahoma. He was there exactly two days – the only two days of schooling he had in his life – when a circus came to town.

The circus owner's 26-year-old daughter took a fancy to the 13-year-old boy. Wareagle went with the circus as the daughter's adopted son and as a "pony boy" – the boy who drove the ponies that drew the monkey's cage. Three years with the circus taught Wareagle how to read and write.

When financial difficulties forced the circus to fold, Wareagle became an oiler on a riverboat. It was in the engine room that he learned to like firewater. He became a heavy drinker at the age of 17 and remained one throughout his life.

Tired of riverboats, Wareagle next became a chauffeur. A trifling incident with his employer caused his temper to flare up and Wareagle quit after three weeks. He rambled through several states, meandering back to Oklahoma.

One night while he was drinking in a cheap hotel, a drunken cattle rustler took a poke at him. Wareagle saw red, drew the pistol he always carried, and killed the rustler where he stood. Thus, at 19, Wareagle was sentenced to life imprisonment and sent to Oklahoma's Micalaster Penitentiary. Eight months later, an influential rancher and family friend obtained a full pardon for him.

Wareagle then got a job as a steam shovel helper on a Kentucky dam project. After three weeks, he got drunk with the boss, shot and killed him in an altercation. For this, he was sentenced to Kentucky's Eddyville Penitentiary for 21 years. Again, a friend came to his aid, this time the contractor on the dam project. Once more, Wareagle was pardoned. The contractor offered him a job as cattle keeper on his Alabama ranch. It was there that Wareagle wooed and wed his first wife, Pearl Roberts.

Some months later, the cattle owned by a neighboring rancher started moseying through a fence and onto the pastures of Wareagle's boss. Wareagle warned the rancher to fix his fence. When the cattle still strayed over the boundary, he shot a steer as a warning. The rancher sent his son to see Wareagle. There were hot words and fisticuffs. Both men pulled out their guns and shot simultaneously. Wareagle's bullet lodged in his opponent's chest, while he was shot in the center of the frontal bone of his head. He claimed he was unconscious for seven days and spent one month in the hospital. Doctors warned that some day his mind would snap as a result of his skull fracture.

No legal action followed the shooting, but Wareagle had painful frontal headaches and severe vertigo for years. Three months after his release from the hospital, his wife died from pneumonia. Wareagle wandered again. He finally landed in a small Tennessee town where he married Ola Duffle, had two children, and became fireman on a railroad. About a year later, the government started paying him $275 every two months as compensation for Indian oil rights. Wareagle continued to receive this sum while he was at Alcatraz. With this money, Wareagle bought a farm and became a cattle rancher. Saturday nights he went into town to get drunk. One night, while returning from town with a large wad of bills, four men waylaid him. Up flared the Wareagle temper again. Undaunted by superior numbers, he fought. During the fracas he was shot – again in the head. Again he lay in the hospital for months. He emerged with a temper more violent and uncontrollable than ever. After a fit of rage, he would streak into town, get drunk, and remember nothing until days later in a hotel, bar, or jail.

He developed amnesia spells, often regaining his memory when he was more than 100 miles from home. The spells, he said, began by a dull headache accompanied by a strong urge to go places – anywhere. He said he became semi-conscious, then started traveling.

He enlisted in the Army for two years, serving in Alabama and Georgia. His amnesia spells continued and his urge for solitude grew. Often he wandered from the barracks and into the woods, escaping discipline because he was under doctor's care. In 1919, he was honorably discharged.

Wareagle seldom remained at home. In 1929, he woke up in an Ohio hotel room with a woman named Grace Hilton. She asked him to take her to a town in Michigan. Wareagle, who claimed he was drunk, did so. He was arrested and sent to Leavenworth for a two-year term for violating the

Mann Act. He spent 19 months of this term in a psychiatric ward.

Wareagle became a narcotics addict after his release. He blamed the doctor who gave him morphine following an appendicitis operation in Leavenworth. His addictions prevented him from holding any job more than a few months. He landed in Atlanta, started peddling dope, but dropped it when he found the business too hot. Once after an angry spat with his wife, he lived in some Kentucky caves for six months. When he returned home, he had another amnesia spell. He was later accused of kidnapping a man, tying him to a tree, and beating the victim severely. But Wareagle said he remembered nothing of this and that a hired man framed him.

Wareagle had a clear view of the water boat from his perch atop the cliffs.

Mass Break

A latent but ever-present fear dogged the civilian population on Alcatraz. It was the fear of a mass prison break that could spew 300 desperate men onto the rocky terraces of the Island – to murder and pillage on their bloody road to freedom. This shadowy terror caused guards to resign, pack up wife and children, and move to a healthier neighborhood.

Experts admitted in whispers that a mass break was possible and that the Rock was not the foolproof lock-up boasted by the government. It was a vulnerable spot, where its civilian population could be captured and held as hostages or shields by frenzied prisoners.

Civilians imagined the prisoners lifting the electric gate of the work area and releasing the entire prison population. True, many of the escapees would be shot in the stampede by prison guards. But prisoners out numbered guards 5 to 1 and, in the eyes of men who had nothing to lose, death was a sweet and easy gamble.

Armed with weapons and tools from the prison workshops, the civilians envisioned the demoniac horde swarming freely over the Island. They would shoot here, kidnap there, or plunge off the cliffs into the surf and swim for freedom.

A gang of prisoners could barricade themselves snugly into one of the civilian dwellings, threaten and commit unspeakable crimes unless promised and given freedom. Or, employing women and children as a protective shield, escapees might gain the prison wharf and commandeer the prison launch or other craft.

Tower guards – if any remained – would not let the melodrama progress too far. They knew the cold, hard law of the Rock. "Shoot any escaping prisoner in spite of danger to any hostages used as a screen." Before quelling a major uprising, flower-terraced Alcatraz might resemble a slaughterhouse stockyard.

This hypothetical prison break became hideous reality on May 23, 1938. Only a bad guess by the prisoners and a pane of shatterproof glass prevented what could have been a violent mass prison break. Tight-lipped prisoners would not divulge to authorities the number of prisoners aware of the plot. But the prison grapevine telegraphed there were scores.

Jimmy Lucas, Thomas R. Limerick, and Rufus Franklin were elected to spring their comrades. All three had long-term prison sentences – Limerick for bank robbery and kidnapping; Franklin for bank robbery, assault, and violation of the National Motor Vehicle Act; Lucas for bank robbery and violating the Dyer Act.

All three prisoners would be stooped and aged before they saw the outside world again. So they figured a scuffle or two, a few quick shots and, if death won, well, it was better than life in a rocky tomb.

Limerick was shot in the head and died in the hospital before midnight the day of the abortive attempt. Before he died, he gasped, "The only thing

I'm sorry about is that I ever let a cop take me in the first place. I wish I had been plugged and killed before I ever came here."

The plot was daring. They were to capture a guard tower after disabling or killing the guard, seize his rifles, guns and ammunition, then make a quick dash for the second tower. This was the tower where the two large prison gates were controlled. Once the gates were open, the victors would sound a signal for the prisoners in the workshops. Workshop prisoners would then attack the guards, scoop up what weapons they could, and run.

It began after lunch when the threesome picked up their unfinished tasks in the second floor model workshop.

The atmosphere was charged with tension. As they hammered and sawed, the other prisoners watched Limerick, Franklin and Lucas and the unsuspecting guard on duty, Rolin C. Cline. Soon the three prisoners rose from their tasks and one by one ambled over to the guard.

"Say, Mr. Cline, that varnish I'm putting on my cabinet is kinda thick and gummy," Limerick remarked affably. "What will I do with it?"

Behind Cline stood Lucas and Franklin. Before the guard could answer, Franklin brutally smashed him over the head with a hammer. As he slumped on the floor unconscious, the three ruffians pelted him with iron missiles from the shop, kicked him and broke his skull in several places. Cline slid into the grave without ever regaining consciousness.

Hammers and saws got louder and busier as the three ringleaders leapt to one of the windows.

Because the distance from the shop to the ground was deemed too high for any man to jump without fatal results, no steel bars were installed outside the windows. But the ground was not their objective. It was the roof.

One of them produced a wooden wedge. It was specially prepared to steady and reinforce the open window so that a man could stand upon it. Franklin carried the bloody hammer with which Cline was bludgeoned, while Limerick and Lucas loaded their pockets with iron scraps and pieces of steel casing for later use.

Before the prisoners ascended to the roof, they had to contend with a projecting barbed wire cornice. But they prepared themselves for that with a wire cutter. Balancing on the open window, Limerick snipped the barbed wire, handed the cutters to Lucas, and then hoisted himself up. Lucas was next, then Franklin. They scuttled over the roof where the guard tower stood – their first offensive. A catwalk leading to the guard tower prevented them from being spotted by the guard.

Harold P. Stites, the guard on duty that day, was recently transferred from Leavenworth. Prisoners learned that the way prisoners do. They knew he was a veteran and a good shot but they also knew he was "green" to the surroundings. They chose that particular time and day because Stites was on the job.

Now the three desperadoes were out in the open. Stites' back was turned as they rushed for the tower. They threw the iron chunks at the glass windows of the tower, hoping to blind the new guard by flying pieces of glass. Stites later admitted he was surprised by the attack. Had he been struck by jagged glass or by the flying missiles, the three might easily have seized him and his weapons. Then the gates would open to the worst prison break in history. This was not conjecture, the prisoners muttered and argued about it afterwards.

But the shatterproof glass windows of the guard tower foiled the plot. That particular tower – with its life-saving shatterproof glass – was built at a later date than the other towers, where the glass was not shatterproof. That was the only thing the escaping trio had not found out beforehand.

Pieces of iron deluged the glass panes. The glass only cracked and splintered, no pieces flew. Stites fired on the escapees through the glass with his automatic 45-caliber pistol. Limerick was shot first. A bullet crashed through his head. He died a few hours later in the prison hospital.

As the excited Stites continued to fire, the remaining two prisoners ducked and dodged his bullets. The guard's pistol was empty when Franklin reached the door of the tower, brandishing his hammer. Stites just had time to reach for his Army Springfield rifle. He leveled it, fired, and Franklin dropped with bullets in his shoulder and lung. He would have rolled off the roof to inevitable death were it not for the barbed wire he and his companions had cut on their way up to the roof. Until they took him to the hospital, the unconscious Franklin hung across the wire like a drooping sack, the bloodstained claw hammer still clutched in his hand.

Now only Lucas was left. He ran like a frightened animal. He dived under the catwalk and crouched there with upraised hands whimpering, "Don't shoot – please don't shoot." This was the "tough" Jimmy Lucas who once stabbed Capone with a scissors blade.

The shooting occurred around 2 p.m. As the prisoners marched back to their cells – like they always were after any kind of a disturbance – they saw the swaying form of Franklin draped over the roof wire. That told them the break failed. A heavy silence hung over the cellblock that night, punctured by frequent mutterings – and the sneeze-knock-and-cough telegraph. But the signals were not altogether those of despair. The three prisoners killed one of the hated "coppers" and that was something.

The deputy warden snapped handcuffs onto the cowering Lucas and took him off the roof. He was dragged through the prison yard and placed in solitary for a long term. Franklin was taken to the prison hospital. Both were later indicted for murder.

Reflections

Editor's Note

After re-reading my father's manuscript in the mid-1980s, I asked him a battery of questions. While reflecting on his responses, he remembered secret stories that could now be safely told. He also reflected on his once naïve attitude toward the prisoners. I am pleased to share my father's reflections with you.

When I first arrived on the Rock, the sick line was very heavy. Many prisoners wanted to meet and size-up the new "saw-bones." Like a pet kitten, I was accepted and "in." I treated the prisoners who required medical care not as cons but as people with an identity. This was my natural attitude. After I was accepted, the prisoners endured personal pain and distress rather than make sick line and possibly be confined to a cell instead of a much-desired yard privilege.

Charles Yanowsky was a patient in the prison hospital for a short time. This incident occurred about four months after my arrival on Alcatraz. I was having some difficulty with my supervisor, Dr. Hess. There was no doubt that he was taking advantage of my good nature. We were the only two doctors at Alcatraz and provided continuous medical coverage. I was always willing to cover for Dr. Hess when he had social obligations or appointments. When I realized that he was taking advantage of me. I refused to cover for him. His requests soon stopped.

Yanowsky found out about my problem through the prisoner grapevine [there were no secrets on Alcatraz].

Yanowsky had lived in the East New York area of Brooklyn. He hung around the poolrooms and gyms where prizefighters trained and often congregated. This was after the turn of the century and during the roaring twenties.

My uncles, Charlie Beecher and Willy Beecher [our name was later changed to Beacher], were well-known professional prizefighters. Willy Beecher also owned and operated Willy Beecher's Gym in East New York. Yanowsky was well acquainted with the Beecher's. One day Yanowsky approached me in the main hospital ward and told me of his connection with the Beecher prizefighters.

I was amused that three thousand miles west of Brooklyn there was someone who knew members of MY family.

"Doc," he said, "I know Dr. Hess is giving you some trouble. Just say the word and I'll see that he is taken care of." Yanowsky later offered to 'take care of' prisoner Ping, who made anti-Semitic remarks in my presence. "You have a lot of friends here," Yanowsky emphasized. I was handling Ping effectively with cold, silent stares and declined his offer once again.

Finding acceptance among the prisoners took many forms – even with personal laundry.

Prisoners washed and ironed all our laundry. Each week we checked off the items being sent to the laundry on a printed laundry list. Prisoners collected the list and our laundry weekly. Personal laundry was frequently returned damaged.

There were some minor incidents to my shirt collar tabs soon after my arrival. Then suddenly the malicious damage stopped. Instead, I was the recipient of new linen handkerchiefs, new articles of apparel, and the best cuts of beef and groceries from the prisoner-operated commissary.

Wareagle was under my care and treatment in the prison hospital for coronary artery heart disease. He almost expired.

Sometime during a recovery phase, he prepared a document and called it his last will and testament. One day, he handed me some papers and told me to read them in private. The papers indicated that I was the beneficiary of something that was very valuable. It was kept in general delivery at a post office in a town somewhere in the Midwest. All I had to do was appear and sign for it and it was mine. I never went to the designated location and never thought about this incident again until now.

I recall an incident during the strike when I visited a prisoner in the dungeon. "Stir," commanded the guard as I approached. The prisoner didn't move. I felt the prisoner was probably defiant because the guard was present. I remember this guard well. He was a hateful bastard and could be mean to prisoners. So, when he asked me to "step around the corner" of the dark, narrow aisle, I responded spontaneously, not knowing what he wanted. I knew something was amiss because he didn't follow me. I retraced my steps and found the guard pummeling and prodding the prisoner through the steel bars with a piece of pipe.

"What are you doing?" I asked him in a tone of disapproval. He stopped, looked at me, and made some improper remark including the words, "By God." We then continued our rounds through the dungeon.

The guard took exception to my disapproval of his actions and reported me to the warden. The warden called me to his office and asked me to explain the incident. I defended myself and heard no more of this incident.

Phil "Red" Ryan was easy to talk to. A friendly type. Fatherly. You would never think of him as a gangster or safecracker.

Ryan was chronically ill and "lived" in the main ward of the prison hospital. We would exchange a few words each day. He approached me one morning after casual amenities and said, "Doc, I have a plant for you."

I would remove my uniform jacket and wear a long white lab coat in the hospital. My lab coat had two front pockets. Well, he took me by surprise and slipped something into my right front pocket.

"Don't doc," he exclaimed. "Not here."

"What did you give me?"

"Not now. Wait until you are on the outside in private. Don't show it to anyone." He seemed concerned and realized how naïve I was.

"OK Ryan," I murmured as I walked away.

As you must know, it was strictly forbidden to take or receive anything from the prisoners.

I returned to my quarters later in the day and examined the content of the little packet. I unfolded the white paper and two flat folded green articles of thumbnail size appeared. I unfolded them and, to my astonishment, two $5 bills appeared. They seemed to be compressed in an oil or wax base. What to do? I applied a heated small hand iron and was able to gradually dry and stretch them to their normal size.

Now I knew what a plant was! I was in possession of something I should not have received. And there was no way in which I could return it. And I certainly would not report the incident to the warden.

The following day in the hospital ward, I approached Ryan when we were alone.

"Ryan," I said, "why did you do that?"

"Forget it, doc," he answered. "I have no use for it here."

"What am I going to do with it? I don't dare give it back to you."

"Forget it – spend it."

We both never mentioned or spoke of the incident again. I kept the $10 well hidden, fearful it would only create trouble for me.

One day I was in the San Francisco train depot en route to Los Angeles and decided to see if the bills were legitimate. I approached the ticket counter, expecting to be apprehended at any moment. I requested my ticket and placed the two bills on the counter. The ticket clerk took the bills and gave me my change and the tickets. I was now forever free of my Alcatraz contraband.

Sometime later, Ryan approached me in the prison hospital. "Doc, I want to ask you for something. But whatever your answer is, please do not be offended."

Again, being naïve, I asked what he had in mind. He explained that there was a package in San Francisco that he wanted me to pick up and deliver to him.

"Do this for me and you can have anything you want – money, cars, jewelry and furs for your wife."

I believe he knew my answer before he finished. Without hesitation, I refused his generous offer.

His last words to me were, "No offense intended doc. I knew you wouldn't accept my offer."

He also knew without saying so that I would not report him to the warden for attempting to bribe me. So, the plant was a prelude for something bigger and better. Thinking about it now, I see how easy it might be for some people to be influenced into an illegal venture for personal gain.

Being young and idealistic, I was treating patients, not criminals. I had no prior prison experience. I also had no fear. I was not fully aware that I was working in a maximum security prison. The prisoners were kept under strict supervision and given very few privileges. At the time, I thought the system was too strict and the prisoners were being dehumanized. In recent years, the pendulum has moved in the opposite direction.

Prisoners and criminals seem to have more rights than victims and families. Murderers live on death row for years with all the conveniences of a good home – clean linens, radios, TVs, magazines, newspapers, and three meals a day. And all this without working for it. And at taxpayer's expense.

Judges and law enforcement officials are far too lenient today. Youthful offenders are frequently released only to commit new and more heinous crimes. This became painfully clear when a youthful offender deliberately and brutally murdered friends in my Florida neighborhood. A judge had recently released him from jail.

I feel criminals must pay for their crimes and must be prohibited from buying leniency.

⋆ ⋆ ⋆

Poems were written in the prisoner's own hand on paper provided by the prison. It was a show of egoism when a prisoner gave me something he wrote. He was also breaking prison rules because this was strictly forbidden. I became, in a sense, a silent partner in a broken rule.

⋆ ⋆ ⋆

Here is an excerpt from my father's handwritten journal that he chose not to include in his manuscript.

Early in the afternoon of the (Roe and Cole) escape, I found the rear basement door of my house open and wondered if the escapees had ventured inside. I searched the Island for the deputy to request a search. I came upon a guard stationed near the parade ground.

"Have you seen Deputy Miller?" I asked.

"No. The warden is right across the parade ground over there," he said indicating the direction.

"What is the warden doing over there by himself?" I wondered as I approached him.

"Warden Johnston."

"Hello, doctor."

"I've been looking for the deputy but I can't seem to locate him."

"What is it?"

"I want my house shaken down. It seems that the rear basement door, which is always closed, is open. The house is huge enough to hide any number of men."

"All right, doctor. I'll get a search party to go through your home and the other homes on the topside. All houses will be thoroughly searched before nightfall," he reassured me.

A peculiar thought crossed my mind as I walked with him along the parade ground around the south end of the Island. A four-foot wall extended all around the parade ground beyond which a steep slope extended to the water's edge. We were 300 feet from the nearest guard and out of sight from the tower guard around the bend.

"Suppose these convicts are crouched behind that wall," I thought. "We could be grabbed as hostages. And orders are to shoot to kill despite the consequences to the warden or anyone else."

"What are the possibilities of their attempt being successful?" I asked.

"It's hard to say. I don't think they can beat that water. In all probability they are drowned."

The night of the escape everyone was ordered to stay indoors and to keep all lights on. Search parties kept busy. They expected shooting.

Many foghorns were heard that day. A woman on the Island said that there was a boat stationed off the north end for several hours. It was sounding its horn.

"It wasn't like other foghorns I have heard before," she said.

Was that boat waiting for the escaped prisoners? Was its foghorn calling them by sound? Did Cole and Roe swim in the direction of that foghorn? Or was it some small craft waiting for the fog to lift?

Did escapees Roe and Cole survive chilly San Francisco Bay?

Reviews from readers like you
are encouraged.

Please contact us at
www.alcatrazdoc.com.

Order Form

ALCATRAZ ISLAND
Memoirs of a Rock Doc

Please ship me _____ books @ $19.95   _____
USA shipping is free for the first book.
$2.00 for each additional book   _____
6% sales tax (New Jersey residents only)   _____
Total enclosed   _____

Name: _____

Address: _____

_____

Email: _____

Please mail your money order to:
    Pelican Island Publishing
    P. O. Box 671
    Lebanon, NJ 08833-2146 USA

For information or international shipping charges, please write to the above address or contact us at www.alcatrazdoc.com.

Reviews from readers like you
are encouraged.

Please contact us at
www.alcatrazdoc.com.

Order Form

ALCATRAZ
ISLAND
Memoirs of a Rock Doc

Please ship me _____ books @ $19.95   _____
USA shipping is free for the first book.
$2.00 for each additional book   _____
6% sales tax (New Jersey residents only)   _____
Total enclosed   _____

Name: _____

Address: _____

_____

Email: _____

Please mail your money order to:
      Pelican Island Publishing
      P. O. Box 671
      Lebanon, NJ 08833-2146 USA

For information or international shipping charges, please write to the above address or contact us at www.alcatrazdoc.com.

Reviews from readers like you
are encouraged.

Please contact us at
www.alcatrazdoc.com.

Order Form

ALCATRAZ ISLAND

Memoirs of a Rock Doc

Please ship me _____ books @ $19.95   _____
USA shipping is free for the first book.
$2.00 for each additional book   _____
6% sales tax (New Jersey residents only)   _____
Total enclosed   _____

Name: _____

Address: _____

_____

Email: _____

Please mail your money order to:
       Pelican Island Publishing
       P. O. Box 671
       Lebanon, NJ 08833-2146 USA

For information or international shipping charges, please write to the above address or contact us at www.alcatrazdoc.com.